D1575479

THE ART OF
★ THE ★
DONALD

LESSONS *From* AMERICA'S
PHILOSOPHER-IN-CHIEF

Christopher Bedford

THRESHOLD BOOKS
New York London Toronto Sydney New Delhi

Threshold Editions
An Imprint of Simon & Schuster, Inc.
1230 Avenue of the Americas
New York, NY 10020

First Threshold Editions hardcover edition October 2017

THRESHOLD EDITIONS and colophon are trademarks of Simon & Schuster, Inc.

For information about special discounts for bulk purchases, please contact Simon & Schuster Special Sales at 1-866-506-1949 or business@simonandschuster.com.

The Simon & Schuster Speakers Bureau can bring authors to your live event. For more information, or to book an event, contact the Simon & Schuster Speakers Bureau at 1-866-248-3049 or visit our website at www.simonspeakers.com.

Interior design by Renato Stanisic

Manufactured in the United States of America

10 9 8 7 6 5 4 3 2 1

Library of Congress Cataloging-in-Publication Data

Names: Bedford, Christopher, author.
Title: The art of the Donald : lessons from America's philosopher-in-chief / Christopher Bedford.
Description: New York : Threshold Editions, 2017.
Identifiers: LCCN 2017037050 (print) | LCCN 2017037612 (ebook) | ISBN 9781501180361 (ebook) | ISBN 9781501180347 (hardback) | ISBN 9781501180354 (trade paper)
Subjects: LCSH: Trump, Donald, 1946—Philosophy. | Leadership. | Industrial management. | Life skills. | BISAC: SELF-HELP / Personal Growth / Success. | PHILOSOPHY / Political. | REFERENCE / Quotations.
Classification: LCC E913.3 (ebook) | LCC E913.3 .B43 2017 (print) | DDC 973.933092—dc23
LC record available at https://lccn.loc.gov/2017037050

ISBN 978-1-5011-8034-7
ISBN 978-1-5011-8035-4 (pbk)
ISBN 978-1-5011-8036-1 (ebook)

THIS BOOK IS DEDICATED TO YOU ALL—
EVEN THE HATERS AND LOSERS.

Contents

Preface

In many, many years, when President Donald Trump is gone, he will leave behind an American brand, a global business empire, a populist moment that changed the planet, and a family that loves him.

When he started in business, he was written off by his competitors. When he rose in city politics, he was written off by local politicians. When he ran for president, he was written off by the news media.

Despite it all, a man without any special skills in acting or singing became the most famous person on the planet. A man whose business troubles and stumbles have been documented for decades became one of its wealthiest. A man dismissed by every class of America's political insiders became her president.

His life—both what he is and how he got here—is a life

worth studying. His style—how he communicates, how he negotiates, how he fights, how he wins—is a style worth understanding. His story is one of taking on incredible odds, and carrying on. It's a story of the fighting spirit.

It's the art of the Donald, and it's an American tale.

The Steakhouse Populist

I got to the Hanover Street Chophouse early on a Monday night.

That day I first met Donald Trump had started in a Holiday Inn in New Hampshire and gone downhill steeply. Clinton campaign staff wouldn't let me into the gymnasium where, after an hour-long line, Bill Clinton was talking about himself on his way toward introducing his wife. Now, instead of sweating it out in a high school gym with the rest of them, I was confined to standing in the hall, watching through a thick glass wall while sixty-something white Democrats grooved terribly atop the bleachers to Latin music. It's unlikely the few Hispanics in the Manchester audience that day were swayed, though I couldn't confirm—I was locked out.

Sick of this unsavory offering, I packed into the driver's seat of a borrowed car and drove with a young reporter through a whiteout blizzard to a stone country church.

There, I found the room was too packed to catch a glimpse of one John Kasich, who had been storming the state, telling everyone who would listen that he was "the Prince of Light," and everyone else was an A-hole.

After a stopover at Anselm College (where I made my Fox *Special Report* debut accidentally wandering on camera, to use a bathroom), a cab ride from a fisherman who was in between voting for Marco Rubio and Donald Trump, and a phone call interrogation from Tucker Carlson's spitfire wife demanding to know if I was supporting Trump or "some squish," I was ready for a glass of bourbon.

That's how I got to New Hampshire's Hanover Street Chophouse early on a Monday night. The day was looking up already.

It's usually a bore to sit at the bar with someone who doesn't drink anymore, but Tucker Carlson often manages to cause enough commotion to get a conversation going with someone more inclined toward the drink, and the bar was buzzing when I asked the maître d' if he got a lot of presidential candidates in his quiet restaurant.

"No, no," he assured me. "They would never be seen in an expensive steakhouse." Terrible optics, of course.

Too bad for them, I thought. Good news for me, with Tucker buying.

After a few more reporters arrived, shuffling out of the cold, we saw a pair of Secret Service agents in long black coats enter, alert.

We've got one, I thought. Manhattan's self-styled enemy of Wall Street, Hillary Clinton, must be breaking the rules and ditching New Hampshire's diners for a little luxury. The headline would write itself. Until it didn't.

Just a few moments later, Donald J. Trump walked through the door with his entire family and ruined any sugarplum headline that had dared dance through my head.

Who cared if Donald Trump, skyscraper billionaire, wanted a nice steak after a long day? Normal rules of politics aside, who among us wouldn't?

He came right up to our table, clapping one reporter by the shoulders and telling the whole group, "This guy is a champ! He never stops working—he works nights, he works weekends, he never stops."

Every one of us knew that was as far from the truth as it could get, and Mr. Trump clearly didn't know this reporter beyond his name, but what a mover. Every pundit on the news had told us The Donald was a cold fish incapable of human warmth, and here we were. As far as warmth goes, it was like sitting next to a furnace.

His sons pulled out their phones and showed me their prize kills from the hunting trail—an impressive gallery a Massachusetts boy had no shot at relating to. But I had played the arcade classic Big Buck Hunter, and when they showed me a particularly massive mountain goat carcass, I bragged I'd achieved the rank of "Buck Hunter Hero" on that very level. Their eyes betrayed worry I was mad, but they were too polite to ask. "Aren't there any pictures of your kids?" I wondered.

"That's exactly what my wife says!" one of them laughed.

Their father, meanwhile, was entertaining the table with stories from the debate two nights earlier. "I was standing near the guy on the debate stage. The guy just sweating and sweating," he said, sharing what was likely not deep-seated concern for Florida's junior senator, Marco Rubio.

"And I was like, 'Hey, are you okay, man?'" he went on, his head cranking to the side, eyes opening wide in a worried expression as authentic as any you'll get.

It was believable. And it was funny.

It didn't even matter that he was a billionaire in a steakhouse in a depressed, former industrial town beset by heroin. It didn't even matter that he ordered his steak well-done and passed on the wine. Our shallow conversations in the dining room had shattered all my TV-derived opinions, even against my strong preference for a man who drinks daily and eats rare meat.

As the sun rose the next morning, I walked alone into a packed diner where Tucker and his cohost Steve Doocy were filming *Fox & Friends,* talking with locals eager for a little camera time and waiting for the steady troop of presidential celebrities sure to swing by.

When I walked in, a booth lay open right beside the set, and I sat down to hold it for a car of sleepy reporters coming in behind me. Jeb Bush was alone at the diner's bar, arms on the table, head sagging, waiting for the hit. With New Hampshire's humans unable to pass through the live set, he was by himself. It could have been a sad painting. He was tired, no doubt, and after his interview he left through a back door.

Chris Christie was next, coming in through the door Jeb had exited, sitting down for a quick hit on the camera and exiting the same.

Then the Secret Service Uniformed Division came in, including one officer so pretty it almost wasn't terrible to have to get my ID checked when I used the restroom. They were protecting Donald Trump again, and while his squirrelly old campaign manager, Corey Lewandowski, buried himself in his smartphone, Trump and Melania jumped into the thick of the crowd.

By the time he finally sat down for a Fox interview, he knew the staff's names. Calling to Sue in the back of the kitchen, he yelled, "Just tell me who are you voting for?"

"America!" she yelled back, to a round of applause.

"I love her!" Trump hollered.

"Make it two eggs, over tremendous!" Tucker laughed.

"And she's seen everybody come in, they've all seen Sue, but she just, I walked in she said, 'Mr. Trump, I'm voting for you.' That's why I asked the question, you think I would have asked the question if I . . . ?"

The segment wrapped up, but an hour later Secret Service was still checking IDs for bathroom users—Donald Trump and his wife were still in a booth, now in the middle of the diner, digging in on a carb-heavy, sweet-toothed breakfast plate and chatting it up with a small audience of New Hampshire voters.

In the sharp suit and the tie, he looked as at home as the folks bundled up in winter jackets and snow boots. He fit right in with a crowd whose combined wealth didn't compare to his own. And he loved it.

Donald Trump walloped the competition that day—not only in doubling the runner-up's votes, but in winning the hearts of the people who met him.

A steakhouse billionaire who was at home with a hot stack in a bright diner was pulling up a chair at Washington, D.C.'s table.

From what he said to what he ate, whom he hired and how he played, Donald Trump broke nearly every rule of American politics. Before he did that, he broke a few in business. And before he's done, he'll likely break a few in the White House.

It's too late for a lot of politicians who doubted the real estate television star, but for the millions of Americans who supported him, there's a lot to learn about living the good life, running your own affairs, building a team, communicating your ideas, dealing with critics, and, finally, winning. Winning so much you get tired of winning.

Let's see if the rest of the country wises up.

1

✫

Building Your Empire, Deal by Deal

Donald Trump is in charge.

There's really no questioning it. When he hit what most of us would call a rough patch—ending his marriage and losing a billion dollars in the 1990s—some wondered if he'd lost his senses, but never if he'd lost control of his business. And even while the newspapers scamper after tidbits of gossip from the most fascinating White House anyone can recall, one thing rings clear: Donald Trump is in charge.

And after decades of bellyaching from reporters and pundits, comic book artists and magazine writers, mayors and presidents, another thing is clear: The man is one of the most effective leaders and impressive managers onstage today.

Donald Trump learned a lot from the successes of his father, Fred Trump, a businessman who made a fortune building affordable housing in New York City's less expensive boroughs. He also learned a lot from the failures of his older brother, Freddy, who lost his life to the bottle. But he learned the most from himself—from a half century of both smart decisions and disastrous mistakes.

Throughout his career, Trump cut out the losers, never wasting time talking to the wrong people. He kept in mind that when he was doing something new, the old rules didn't apply. He remembered that you don't need most of the people who say you need them. He sought leverage at every moment, with a mind always on the deal. He used all resources available, confounding and countering foes with more time, money, and access. And the whole time, he lived his brand, from his books to his show, from his hotels to his condos, and from Manhattan to D.C.

The last president said, "If you've got a business, you didn't build that." His successor disagrees.

Donald Trump didn't just build a global business empire out of his father's more modest real estate fortune: He forged one of America's strongest brand names; he created one of the country's most popular reality shows; and, from the ground up, he built the greatest insurgent political campaign ever seen.

He built all of that, and he did it his way, with a few rules of his own making. Trump is not a businessman; he's an empire builder on every level.

The funny thing is, despite everything he'd accomplished, none of the people who fancy themselves in charge expected Donald Trump to win the presidency.

In June 2016, around the time she became the presumptive Democratic candidate for president, the "failing" *New York Times* gave Hillary a 58 percent chance of winning the election. It was the lowest chance they gave her the entire time they charted her course against Trump, with her chances peaking at 93 percent in late October and resting at 85 percent on the morning of Election Day.

The company *Newsweek* contracts to create its commemorative issues sent the "Madam President" cover far and wide. A framed copy hangs in the Daily Caller News Foundation's office.

And naysayers weren't relegated to Democrats and their media adjuncts. The week leading up to Election Day, in an attempt to save face before the crushing defeat they assumed was coming, the Republican National Committee invited reporters to an off-the-record briefing on just how they expected to lose.

It's hard to blame them. Everyone the RNC cared to listen to was in Washington, and everyone in Washington who "mattered" was saying the same thing. The fear of being an apostate is very real in this city, and the effect of all the same opinions being voiced in unison all around you is akin to standing in the middle of a tornado—there may be a world outside it, but it doesn't seem to matter right then, does it? The certainty of Trump's imminent annihilation was so great, a Princeton election forecaster vowed to eat a bug if the tycoon triumphed. Nate Silver of FiveThirtyEight was targeted by a *Huffington Post* hit piece for daring to say Trump had a real chance.

The night of November 8, on the way between the Javits Center's sea of Hillary hipsters and Facebook's New York headquarters, where we were filming a live shoot, our team stopped off at an Italian joint. The night had been long and frustrating, like most trips to that city end up when you're sober enough to care. The first results from Florida were coming in and they looked ugly for Trump.

I was hoping in vain the drink I ordered would improve my spirits while going through our schedule in what figured to be an agonizing night of gloating by elite journalists and the Beltway set. Then, suddenly, Blake Neff, our education writer, who was the closest thing we had to a data analyst, perked up.

"It's happening."

"What is?" I asked. I don't remember if I even looked up.

"I'm not positive . . . but it really looks like Trump is going to win Florida."

It wasn't supposed to happen that way, the people who thought they were in charge said, wailing and rending their garments.

But Donald Trump hadn't asked their permission.

RULE 1: Go Straight to the People Power Comes From. In Business, the Boss; in Elections, the People.
New York City, with all its five boroughs, is the nerve center of the country. Manhattan is the center of the nerve center. In business, it's the center of the world. So simply being a rich

businessman in an outer borough, as his father was, was not enough for a young Donald Trump: He wanted to be the king of Manhattan.

Trump learned this early on. When he was just a young punk from Queens, his most formidable talent was his gumption and a drive to make it in Manhattan.

He still worked in Brooklyn, but he knew the first order of business was getting an apartment on the island. Step two was to join the club where he knew all the movers and shakers, rich men and beautiful women, spent their evenings. Fake-it-till-you-make-it kind of thing.

Now, any club worth its salt is not going to let a nobody in without the right connections, and Trump didn't know a soul. The first time he called the front desk, they hung up on him because he didn't know anyone on the ins. The second time, they told him there was no shot they were giving him a list of members—that information simply wasn't public. The third call, he stretched the truth a tiny bit and managed to get a phone number for one of the few public members—the top dog, Le Club's president.

He didn't call the front desk a fourth time. No need. Le Club's president, of course, asked him the same questions about who he knew, but the president was a decision maker—a man empowered to make the call he chose. He was as skeptical as the guy at the front desk, but as Trump puts it, "I just kept talking and talking, and finally this fellow said to me, 'I'll tell you what, you sound like a nice young man, and maybe it would be good to have some younger members, so why don't you meet me for a drink at Twenty-One?'"

As it turned out, "a drink" was not in any way singular, and as the weeks passed after their meeting, Trump came to realize his host couldn't even recall the evening, so he would have to try again. But now he wasn't wasting time with middle management; he was aiming for the top of the stack, and it was worth the effort. It paid off, and while he didn't drink, he was a loud admirer of successful men and beautiful women, and a good time was had by all. He'd taken his first step into a whole new social scene without knowing a single person on the list.

One of life's very many oddities is that while everyone hates a middleman, near everybody fancies themselves essential. It's no different at the neighborhood bar or top boardroom: Figuring out who you actually need to talk to is one of life's most essential skills. Not only can it change the amount of time and effort you put into everything from ordering a beer to buying a tower, but it can make the difference in whether you win or lose.

But the trick, in both big and small cases like joining a club or building a hotel, isn't simply to remove the middlemen in between yourself and the target: It's representing yourself, and everything you are in the deal you personally want to make happen. As a reluctant press has come to learn, especially over the first year of his presidency, no one represents

Donald Trump better than himself. It's clear he knows it, too, just as he did then.

"It comes down to the fact that everyone underneath the top guy in a company is just an employee," Trump writes in *The Art of the Deal*. "An employee isn't going to fight for your deal. He's fighting for his salary increase, or his Christmas bonus, and the last thing he wants to do is upset his boss. So he'll present your case with no real opinion."

That employee isn't going to fight for the deal. No one fights for you like you will fight for yourself, except for probably your mom. And by around the time you're getting in trouble in high school, it's already not a great idea to have your mom represent you.

In politics, there may be a different set of players, but just like in business, it's often the man on top who counts, while excitable interns, self-impressed political hires, and puffed-up think tankers rarely matter as much as they insist they do.

In global diplomacy, the do-it-yourself instinct Trump lives by can even backfire. When Russia-connected opposition research was pitched to the campaign, an experienced politico would have sent a lawyer. Having sat in plenty a room hearing about "oppo" from folks pitching it as a story, there's no such thing as not-totally-sketchy oppo, and even by that already low bar, the Russian government name-drop sets off loud alarms.

Donald Trump's son, Don Jr., didn't send a lawyer, though:

He did the opposite, gathering the campaign principals—campaign manager Paul Manafort and Jared Kushner—and putting them in the room with a possible spy. A possible spy who, it later turned out, was a former Soviet counter-intelligence officer.

A former Rubio contractor at a beer garden the next day was astounded. Rubio's top guys would never, he told me, have been in that room on the first meeting. The Trump family, however, is different from the average D.C. politico. If it's important, it's worth doing yourself, they maintain. International dirty business, they learned in a particularly painful lesson, isn't always the same. And in international intrigue, all lessons are lessons hard learned.

Then, sometimes, the top guy isn't who it at first appears. In the royal courts of the past and the administrations of today, you could know a thousand day laborers, but it was your personal relationship with the king and his lords that gave you your power. In an election year, Trump knew, that isn't the case: The real power in an election year is to talk to the people at large—not any one lord or court jester.

The Republican Party has a long tradition of not bucking the power structure. The people who win the nomination are often the next in line. The Richard Nixons, the George H. W. Bushes, the Bob Doles, the John McCains. Notice that the chances of winning the general election aren't widely affected by this succession obsession: It's just the way it's decided.

But in 2016, while a dozen qualified governors and senators jockeyed for the approval of the middle managers at the Republican National Committee and other campaign power structures, Trump identified a different block—a block courted by outside candidates like Ronald Reagan before, but in 2016, once again forgotten: the American people.

Who knew how loud the "silent majority" would get?

When Trump first began his presidential run, coming down a golden escalator, pundits who'd never met him told the country he wouldn't be able to communicate with the average voter. So he did.

In small New Hampshire diners, he bonded without having to kiss a bunch of strangers' babies. In rallies completely lacking the famous celebrities and terrible-but-popular bands Democrats frequently roll out, he got the crowd riled up on his personality alone, making his own case himself. And on the news, with no shot at a fair shake from simpering reporters or prattling opinion makers, he repeatedly made the news himself, nearly forcing networks to allow him to make his case in his own words on televisions the world over.

Traveling around the country, there was little more boring than listening to Marco Rubio tick through the same stump speech in high schools across Iowa. There were few things more distressing than aging Hillary supporters dancing badly to Hispanic music in snowy New Hampshire. And there was nothing as exciting as a Trump rally. Even if the introduction came from Jerry Falwell Jr. (decidedly not a public speaker . . .)

and even when Trump was tired—and he sometimes was—the crowd of veterans, bikers, families, and hecklers kept going. And the cameras rolled.

And the world couldn't get enough. Two networks from Sweden contacted one of our Daily Caller News Foundation reporters in an attempt to bring on a bilingual writer who might have a shot at explaining to their hungry readers what was going on. A reporter from the *Hindustan Times*, a massive paper in India, told me the hunger for Trump news on the other side of the planet was insatiable.

Trump took out the middlemen and even a lot—though not all—of the idiot political handlers who swarmed over Rubio and Jeb! like irritable wasps. There were no rope barricades held up by adoring interns desperate to keep parade crowds from sparking up a conversation. Sure, Trump's rallies were often staffed by a special strain of bozos who looked like oddly shaped extras from a cheesy mafia movie, but besides chasing us reporters around the rally to try to herd us into cages, they could be ignored, and one time, all it took to escape a particularly worthless handler was running into the bathroom and losing the tie. Ties, you see, are a dead giveaway for press at a rally ninety minutes outside Des Moines.

"But the consultants didn't think we would win," he told the Conservative Political Action Conference a few weeks after he was sworn in. "But they all underestimated the power of the people—you. And the people proved them totally wrong. Never—and this is so true, and this is what's been happening—never underestimate the people. Never. I don't think it will ever happen again."

Trump's approach to primary politics, and his removal of most of the goons, made voters feel like he was talking with them. And he was. And despite being a billionaire from Manhattan, he was also getting a lot of the same news as them, speaking the same language.

In the months since he was sworn in, shows like *Fox & Friends* and *Tucker Carlson Tonight* have learned that the president is watching. He, just like the rest of us, is getting his news not simply from compiled dossiers, but from cable TV, the *New York Times, New York Post, Daily Caller.* The latest ten-thousand-word think piece in the *New Yorker* might tickle a few fancies in cocktail circles in Washington and San Francisco, but that kind of high-mindedness isn't read by real Americans, nor are there any signs it's read by the new president.

You and I likely don't have much danger of finding ourselves as isolated as a billionaire who had an executive series of Cadillac limousines named after him, but the danger is still there. The keys are understanding who you're dealing with—who makes the calls at the companies, in your town, in your state—and speaking the same language as them because you understand the things they hear, the things they want, the things you can bring, and why you're the best person to do it.

If you know the correct audience, understand what makes them tick, and make the right case, you can win the deal.

Oh, and know the rules. Or better yet, make your own.

RULE 2: If You're Doing Something New, the Old Rules Don't Apply

If you're doing something completely new, the first thing you might consider is killing all the consultants. Because really, they're the worst.

What we're talking about is the chattering class. The wise men who've been here for decades. Men like Republican pollster Neil Newhouse.

In the days leading up to Governor Mitt Romney's loss to Obama, Newhouse told Ann Romney she'd better start looking for new D.C. housing for her horses—she and Mitt would be moving to the White House. Just a month or so later, only weeks after Election Day, Newhouse was spotted again, this time whispering sweet nothings into Governor Jeb Bush's ear at a fancy hotel in D.C.

Despite having no idea where his last boss stood in the votes—which was, by the way, Newhouse's only job—he failed upward, meeting a new boss for the next contract. And when Jeb Bush went toe-to-toe with Donald Trump a few years later, well, it was back to the unemployment line (for a day or two). Consultants and other professional advice givers, you can be sure, will always take care of themselves, so don't you worry about them.

Mitt Romney's campaign may have been a massive loss for Republican voters, but it was one helluva win for some of the outside firms he contracted to run his fund-raising, advertising, targeting, and other operations. American Rambler Productions, for example, pulled in $155.9 million. Firms called SJZ and Victory Group gobbled up another $22 million. Targeted Victory, which "ran testing and automatization" for the campaign, raked in $96.4 million.

"We didn't do any real targeting on emails until the last two months of the campaign," Aaron Ginn, a Silicon Valley guy who worked for the company during the campaign, told me shortly after the dust settled. "And when we did, targeting was really broad, like 'Do you live in this state?' Not 'When was your last engagement with the website,' 'What was your last donation,' 'When was the last time you volunteered?'"

That didn't stop Targeted Victory from attending the "Pollie Awards," of course. The Pollies, for the vast majority of the planet who haven't heard of them, are an award given by the American Association of Political Consultants to, well, consultants who pay to be considered—all "to honor the 'Best of the Best' in political advertising and communications."

Targeted Victory scooped up thirty-five "Pollie Awards" for their work in 2012, despite not living up to either of the two words that make up its name.

In industries like finance, entertainment, and tech, there's a bottom line that is so easy to uncover, it will run a man out of house and home even if he does his best to ignore it. In politics, not so much.

Just a few years later, it's worth remembering that Jeb! Bush scared the aforementioned Mitt Romney out of running for president by—wait for it—promising to outspend him.

In total he didn't, of course, because he didn't win the nomination, but it was not for lack of trying. Jeb! spent about $125 million on consultants during his campaign, which made it to all of three states, in none of which he even placed in the top three.

"With apologies to Winston Churchill," the *Washington Post* wrote in a rare show of cleverness, "the tale of the Jeb Bush campaign might be summarized as 'Never before have so few spent so much to achieve so little.'"

None of the favorite GOP consultants signed on to Mr. Trump's brash, outsider campaign, of course. They all—the good, the bad, and the in between—went for tried Republican favorites like Jeb!, Marco Rubio, and John Kasich.

But to be fair, why wouldn't they have? Their skills were all based on past contests, and the big payouts they hoped those skills would earn were reliant on a win. None of us thought Trump had a great chance to win; Bush, Rubio, Kasich—these men held a lot more promise by any historic measurement. And even if some people didn't have that feeling in their gut, all they had to do was turn on the TV to see their consultant friends and colleagues agreeing with each other in one big echo of self-affirmation.

"What separates the winners from the losers is how a person reacts to each new twist of fate," Trump tweeted in September 2014.

If Trump's plan was to follow their rules and play by past contests, it would be crucial to bring on old players. But what if that wasn't his plan? What about when the game you want to play is a new one? Or simply a far-improved one?

Years ago, when Southwest Airlines was struggling to improve its performance, its leaders started by contrasting their approach with other airlines, setting goals based on the competition. The only problem was, as most Americans can attest, the other airlines were just as terrible. So Southwest went outside the airline industry, studying NASCAR pit crews—folks whose job was as competitive as it gets, and whose skills were watched by millions on high-stress television. The study worked, and in 2014, *Performance* magazine reported that the company that used to benchmark itself against other companies was now the standard to measure the others by.

The same went for Trump, who was running a new kind of campaign and couldn't afford to benchmark his success against the guys he was intending to beat out.

Take advertising. All the consultants knew that paid television was key to a winning campaign. It had been since the 1960s. And crucially, a lot of these consultants take a cut for the television ads a candidate makes. It's actually common to see the TV guys at the throats of the analytics guys who try to say "this isn't working."

"Of course it's working, we just need more of it," the consultants maintain. And it's more money in their pockets. Despite the campaign's utter failure, Jeb Bush's consultants still walked away with that $125 million, most of which was spent on ads. The eggheads call this "perverse incentives."

And if you pull your head out of the political clouds, you'll know the average American doesn't remember the ads—they remember the famous moments like "Tear down this wall!" They remember the outbursts like "I am paying for this microphone, Mr. Green!" Both of those came, of course, courtesy of Ronald Reagan, a veteran of the big screen with a great sense of the dramatic. Donald Trump, a veteran of the small screen, gave the public plenty of the same sound bite and viral-ready content, dominating airwaves for weeks and months with each utterance—even if that utterance looked like trouble.

Writing in *The Art of the Deal* about one of his regrets from his younger days, Trump recalls the outrage after he tore down famous art deco friezes from the old Bonwit Teller building to make way for the construction of Trump Tower. After admitting that, "[f]rankly, I was too young, and perhaps in too much of a hurry," he adds, "Ironically, the whole controversy may have ended up being a plus for me in terms of selling Trump Tower."

That's because the stories that hit the papers bleeding with outrage over his perceived greed would often begin by classifying that this destruction was "to make way for one of the world's most luxurious buildings."

Now, that is good advertising. And with free buys on the pages of newspapers around the region, sales shot up.

No magazine, TV pundit, or self-help guru would tell you to do this, and Donald Trump himself says he wouldn't try it again, but the incident shows the imperfection of the art, and just how little even the experts understand. Similarly, when, in your gut, you know something really will work, why trust the guys who get it wrong so often?

Jeb Bush had the big-name consultants and the heavy ad buys, but how did that work out? As Trump himself noted after the New Hampshire primary: "Jeb Bush spent more than $40,000,000 in New Hampshire to come in 4 or 5, I spent $3,000,000 to come in 1st. Big difference in capability!"

Of course, many things taken together make up "capability," but Trump's New Hampshire victory was most definitely a product of his natural skill and direct message more than any high-powered strategy.

In the end, Donald Trump spent comparably little on TV throughout the whole campaign. After the election, he'd been outspent by Hillary and her allies by $380 million, according to the *International Business Times*. After the Supreme Court ruled that political spending by outside groups was protected by the First Amendment, liberal consultants worried that whoever spent the most money would always win the presidency, and the rich would steal the votes from the poor. A billionaire proved them wrong, winning working-class white voters with less money spent than the career Democrat.

And instead of benchmarking his political success on political money raised and television ads bought—a field he was severely disadvantaged in—he remade the rules and measured himself against the entire airways, working to dominate the news with his bombast.

And what about being a billionaire? All the consultants say you need to come across as one of the guys, and that's probably true. But a quick look at Romney's campaign shows a wealthy son of a governor doing everything he could to hide who he really was. It was obviously fake, and it rubbed seemingly everyone the wrong way. Donald Trump could walk into that diner in New Hampshire with an expensive suit on and fit right in because he was comfortable in his skin.

It's true, Trump could have used some of Romney's discipline. Even if you think bad coverage has its benefits, the amateur politician committed unforced errors someone could have avoided by talking over and planning his responses.

No one checks Trump's tweets before he shoots them out. This has proved itself a constant worry for his communications team, but has given the authentic Donald Trump direct connection—past his political handlers and the media—to the American voters. By contrast, it was famously reported that it took twenty-two people to approve a Romney tweet.

Better to be yourself and take the hits than move at a sluggish pace, neutered by consultants, politicos, experts, and hacks.

Being comfortable as yourself is the key to this. The criticism directed at politicians like Ted Cruz, Marco Rubio, Paul Ryan, and Mitt was often that they'd changed: They'd gotten more conservative or more liberal, had switched what they stood for on the road to Washington. While criticism of Trump was more likely to focus on how he was a tough businessman or straight talker who spoke crudely in the past—just like he is now—he also took a good deal of flak for flip-flopping. How he handled it was masterful.

When critics hit on changes in his position, from a liberal New Yorker to head of the Republican Party, he didn't get into tongue-twisted, consultant-invented, focus-group-tested explanations—he simply said that what he'd done was what a businessman in New York needed to do. He'd been a businessman in New York for as long as Americans had known of him, so the story checked out.

"Before this I was a businessman," he said in a Republican debate. "I give to everybody. You know what? When I need something from them—two years later, three years later—I call them, they are there for me."

None of the Republicans onstage with him disagreed, though Rubio complained he'd given money to his Democratic opponent.

"With Hillary Clinton, I said, 'Be at my wedding.' And

she came to my wedding. You know why? She had no choice because I gave."

Instead of being neutered by the consultants, he'd just neutered the critics. That's right, he'd said. I did that because I'm the boss. It was incredible to see. Consultants across the political spectrum were flabbergasted. How could it be that so many excellent politicians had been crucified on crisscrossed pairs of flip-flops in years past, but Trump could just shrug them off as part of the job?

Part of the way is showing no fear or weakness, even for a second. "You can't be scared," he wrote on confrontation. "You do your thing, you hold your ground, you stand up tall, and whatever happens, happens."

It was ironic to see Mitt Romney, author of the political manifesto *No Apology: The Case for American Greatness,* seeming so consistently apologetic for his own successes. Trump, on the other hand, promised to "make America great again" and, in a break from traditional politics, never apologized—even when he changed his mind, and even when a lot of folks would say he was dead wrong.

Another key component is not faking it. People can tell when someone pretends to be something the consultants think he ought to be, and they don't like it. That doesn't just go for voters, that goes for your friends, colleagues, bosses.

Most of us don't have teams of professional political consultants telling us what to do or how to be, but we do have constant nagging from folks who say they know better, whether it's glossy fashion magazines and television pundits, or colleagues and competitors.

But there are people out there worth consulting. Among them, the folks closest to the challenge instead of the folks who benefit from you spending on their solutions. When he looked to buy property, Trump always asked "the people who live nearby about the area—what they think of the schools and the crime and the shops," he writes. "I ask and I ask and I ask, until I began to get a gut feeling about something. And that's when I make a decision."

It stands in contrast to the way a lot of decisions are made in Washington. In D.C., it's a common sight to see a panel on the plight of America's workers with, say, a think tank expert or two and a politician. I've had a lot of free lunches and seen a lot of lovely cheese spreads at these events, but the closest thing I've seen to an American worker was the workingman television host Mike Rowe.

Polls and surveys and columns and commercials are good and fine, but they're no replacement for on-the-ground intelligence. And the people in D.C. were completely baffled by the rise of Donald Trump.

Over glasses of bourbon a few weeks ago, one of the smartest D.C. consultants I know shared an off-the-record story on how Trump was going about picking one of his cabinet secretaries. "He's asking random people, he's asking people he meets!" the man exclaimed. He was mortified. There were, after all, hundreds of experts actually qualified to weigh in on this sort of question. The kind that usually staff presidential transitions, insulating their candidate with a thousand white papers and expert opinions.

Why would Trump ask the public about one of their cabinet secretaries? Why would he shoot from the hip?

A few weeks later, Rick Perry was easily confirmed as secretary of energy by the U.S. Senate. The people in D.C. didn't get it. Trust yourself, trust the people on the ground, solicit opinion from every source, and do what you know to be right. Don't apologize for it.

And please fire the consultants.

RULE 3: You Don't Need Most People, Even the Ones Everyone Says You Need

Consultants aren't the only ones. Few folks have as much power as they say, and most people have only as much as you give them. That may seem obvious when you're at your job looking at the guys in Washington, D.C., but partially, that's because it's easier to see landscape at a distance. If you're a human (if not, please ping me online—I would love to break that story) in an even moderately complex society, there are people all around you doing the same.

In Washington, a lot of the guys you'd hang out with from the Pentagon are convinced they're Jason Bourne, and a lot of the guys you wouldn't hang out with at the Environmental Protection Agency are convinced the oceans will drown us if the government shuts down on a Thursday. Of course, neither is true. The guys who are big deals don't tell you (unless they're a Navy SEAL, which are big deals who will tell you), and the EPA is where people who wish they were at the Department of Energy go.

There was little more enjoyable than the few days that Ted Cruz, Mike Lee, and Rand Paul "shut down" the government. Never mind that the government "shuts down" on weekends and holidays (try mailing a postcard); the best part was all the guys who'd claimed they were Bourne texting their buddies to grab a beer midafternoon. 'Twas a two-week vacation for them.

Some of them were obvious, but others aren't so easy to see. Take the president of Hyatt: In *The Art of the Deal,* Trump says he never thought too highly of him, but in the telling of the time, it's clear Trump thought highly enough of him to pitch deals his way for weeks. It was because of the title, of course, and the power we'd assume comes with it. Who would want to be president in name only? But in business, politics, and life, titles can be deceiving.

Part of that is because titles are free. A friend who helped edit this book for me turned out to be pretty darn good at his job, but the way he first earned the title "senior reporter" was picking up a case of beer and not leaving for a higher-paying gig. The rule is, so long as someone doesn't screw up or abuse what you give them, a title can keep them happy.

In my years as a reporter, one thing I've learned is that

"senior editor," for example, means "this guy doesn't really do that much." But a lot of the power a title bestows comes from respect—a respect that Donald Trump showed time and time again he doesn't have for people who don't deserve it.

One of the greatest things Barack Obama did for his party was destroy a generation of his party's consulting class—a class that, along with their Republican counterpart, is among the worst offenders when it comes to exaggerating its own importance. They cling to the sides of political parties like barnacles on old, slow-moving boats. When a politician wins, consultants take the credit. If the candidate loses, consultants blame the candidate and scrape it off their resume—a task far easier than scraping barnacles off the hull.

So how did Obama destroy a whole ship of them? He simply took a different boat. While the Democratic consulting class and all manner of other sea life latched their livelihoods "with Her"—one Senator Hillary Rodham Clinton—the underdog from Illinois recruited from a different set of young people, outsiders, and loyal Chicagoans. And when the Good Ship Hillary went down, the future president had the luxury of choosing who was good enough to bring to the White House and who should be exiled to TV punditry.

And so it was with the businessman from Queens.

On a primary debate stage full of men and women whose titles commanded respect, he called bull—and that was on people who'd accomplished real things in life, at least as far as politicians can.

"Jeb Bush's campaign thinks George W. Bush is its not-so-secret weapon in next Saturday's pivotal primary," a February 2016 *Politico* article began. "Donald Trump couldn't care less."

How little did he care?

"While Donald Trump was building a reality TV show, my brother was building a security apparatus to keep us safe," Jeb Bush said, in a clearly practiced attack. "And I'm proud of what he did," he said to cap it off, looking mighty pleased with Jeb. Then "the kill shot":

"And he's had the gall to go after my mother . . ."

But Trump interrupted, speaking over the higher-voiced governor: "The World Trade Center came down during your brother's reign." The boos from the debate audience were quick.

"Remember that," Trump added, seemingly unfazed. Bush didn't even pivot. "Let me finish," he said, working on his "don't attack my mom" talking point. "He's had the gall to go after my mother . . ."

"That's not keeping us safe," Trump said, not even listening.

"Everything we know about political strategy suggests that Trump's decision to attack George W. Bush will backfire," opined the man famous for running Bobby Jindal's campaign. Jindal's 2016 experience reached its peak at 6 percent in an Iowa opinion poll. He dropped out before the primaries began, but before he did, he distinguished himself by filming a push-up contest for *BuzzFeed,* a liberal website for dumbs.

"If it doesn't backfire, then it will be official; nothing can stop him," a "GOP strategist" told the site, and among his peers, that strategist was far from alone in thinking this. Nearly the entire class of D.C. insiders was appalled. "He's done for!" they crowed. And then Trump won South Carolina, beating second-place Rubio by 10 points—and more than quadrupling Bush's share.

In the 2016 primary, he was on to the donors, lobbyists, and special interests' game, and even the boos wouldn't sway him. "The crowd was on my side except for they were all donors, and lobbyists and special interests," he famously told the cameras.

That isn't to say Trump didn't pay attention to a few people he shouldn't have. His former campaign manager, Corey Lewandowski, was as bad as any of the consultants any campaign had ever hired. He didn't even have a record of winning campaigns: The last campaign he had run—a New Hampshire primary race for Senator Robert Smith—led to the first time in a decade a sitting senator had lost a reelection primary. But like a younger Trump trying to hustle his way into a club he had no business being invited to, Lewandowski got Trump's ear and told him he was the best there was. No one sells a person better than themselves, and it worked— until it was time to deliver.

Stretching the truth is a small sin we're all guilty of. Lord knows Trump does it. Whether it's amping up a good story to your friends or trying to get a job, you're going to downplay the bad parts and play up the good. It's when exaggeration is your living that it's a problem. And it's when those folks who spin yarns spin you into their yarn that it's a problem for you. Pay attention to what they claim, and how they perform: If they get close to you, it shouldn't be for long. Trump is famous for giving smack talkers a chance, and firing them quickly if their smack talk comes up dry.

And then there's the set of people who never even offered to deliver until they needed something. The self-appointed guardians of Washington did everything they could to destroy Trump, and then once he beat them and proved he didn't need any of them, they were shameless enough to ask for a job in the White House.

"They are some of the biggest names in the Republican national security firmament, veterans of past GOP administrations who say, if called upon by President-elect Donald Trump, they stand ready to serve their country again," one *Washington Post* sob story begins, using the word "serve" like it's a substitute for "want a cool job." "But their phones aren't ringing. Their entreaties to Trump Tower in New York have mostly gone unanswered.

"Their transgression," the article points out, is signing on to the public "Never Trump" letters, one of which was put out by the *New York Times*, which hasn't endorsed a Republican for president since Ike, and even endorsed Walter

Mondale. "Transgression" is a funny word to describe calling the guy you want a job from "erratic," "fundamentally dishonest," and "dangerous" to the country.

"They're seeing how it goes and trying to provide advice, counsel, support to our friends who go into the administration," said John Bellinger, a Bush lawyer who busied himself with fighting conservatives in the Bush administration but now organizes public letters he probably regrets.

He was right, of course. In the first year of his presidency, and likely beyond, the never-Trumpers who were too quiet to be easily identified have sabotaged him every step of the way.

But most of us are not in Donald Trump's position—a billionaire who seems to get along with his kids and even his ex-wives. He doesn't really need much, and he's allowed to call it as he sees it. Calling it as you see it any time and every time, in fact, seems to be a privilege afforded only the ultrawealthy. But we don't really need to publicly call it; we just need to identify it correctly, and act accordingly.

When the boss tells you you're nothing and you need him, the chance that he's wrong—and you actually don't need him—is very high. And when you start to think your lawyer, your stockbroker, and importantly, your doctor are essential, look for a second opinion. The wrong people in the wrong places can hold you back and cost you money, success, and even your health. Even the advice of good friends should be judged on its merits, taking a friendship and their accomplishments into consideration but not letting those blind you.

Based on the resumes running against him—governors, senators, doctors—Trump should have taken their advice and quit. But he took one look at what they'd done in their lives—and for this country—and decided against it. He didn't need them.

Still, most of them now want a job. It's funny how that works. National security experts who once seemed so big when they signed their names to public essays calling Donald Trump mentally unstable and unfit to serve seem so small, all of a sudden. It turns out their names were "big" only in Washington, and their power was built entirely on the perception of its existence. To see the crocodile tears pouring forth from the *New York Times* and the *Washington Post* over how dangerous it is to American security to not have Bush-era national security experts back at the Pentagon, you'd start to think they'd been fans of George W. instead of having been the constant critics they were.

There's no need to go into the story of the emperor who had no clothes: It's cliché. But it is a cliché because it has been told for centuries—and it's been told for so long because it still applies.

There's a point to it, too. The Bush team is infamous for starting the war in Iraq for a pretty questionable reason but earns an honorable mention for being unable to secure Afghanistan. A large number of the Bush administration veterans attacking the president didn't just lack actual power—they didn't deserve it.

And even the reporters so used to being taken seriously no longer are. How many Americans have a wife, husband, sister, or brother who used to think there was no newspaper bias before 2016, and now sees it for what it is? When you show that someone who says they're important actually isn't, you don't just win for yourself, you sometimes liberate a whole lot of other clients, customers, and bosses who'd been afraid to call it what it was.

They'd been afraid because it isn't always easy. If it was, more of us would do it, but it's hard, and if you're wrong, well, you lose that round. But it's important. When you're at the bottom trying to get that deal or that promotion, or move to the next part of life, it can be a wall between you and winning. And even once it looks like you've won, the "essential people" can pull you back down to the bottom. Look at all the broke famous athletes and celebrities, running out of more money than you'd imagine you could spend in a lifetime.

But it's when you're down, working to get up, that it can the most dangerous. It can definitely be easier to quietly pursue another angle with a different client, and avoid any public confrontation, than to, say, call out the big man's brother in front of the whole company.

Like Donald Trump, keep your foes at arm's length and don't hit them publicly unless you need to. And if you need to—and hey, sometimes you do—make sure you're ready to win.

THE ART OF THE DONALD ★ 37

Archimedes, the ancient Greek mathematician who died more than two hundred years before Christ, said that with a long enough lever, you can move the planet. And in the words of The Donald, a few millennia later, make sure you have the leverage.

RULE 4: Always Seek Leverage

You can represent yourself, and your interests, in negotiations. You can go straight to the people whom power comes from. You can do something new and make your own rules along the way. You can identify who you need and who you don't, then act accordingly. But even with all of that, you won't sell anyone on anything unless you have something they want.

Sometimes you won't have much, and you'll have to make do with a phone number and some guts. When Donald Trump wanted in on Le Club, it was all gumption. He had no guarantee he would succeed, but he pulled it off. But while gumption can get you into Le Club, it isn't enough to get into the White House. You've got to have more: You've got to have leverage.

Leverage isn't complicated. When you're stuck in traffic in the city and nearly out of gas and the guy on the corner lot is charging fifty cents more a gallon than you want, he's got the leverage. He might not be a billionaire or a politician, he's simply got one up on you—he's got what you need. And you're going to pay him. Or maybe you won't, but when it comes to risking running out of gas in a car with the family in the back, most of us will make that mistake only once.

Like with Archimedes moving the globe, it's a concept that can be expanded without limit.

Sometimes you can create leverage with what you have in your own hand. Like when Donald Trump had a site, construction crews, and an ever-elusive gambling license in Atlantic City. A lot of people before him had acquired some of those things, but few had acquired all. *Playboy* had failed, *Penthouse* had failed, and even some of the major players had come in hundreds of millions over budget. Determined not to go this route, Trump secured financing before he began construction.

Gambling was legalized in Atlantic City in 1978. But within a few short years, the city's reputation as a grave of entrepreneurs was spreading and construction had slowed down massively. That gave a guy willing to build the leverage to demand a quick approval, and he got it. Once he had it, he was able to move to the next part of the deal, and when Holiday Inn approached him with tens of millions of dollars in exchange for the chance to run the place and a share of the profits, it was his call to stay or go.

But sometimes you don't have the leverage you need, and it takes a little cleverness.

One of Trump's first major deals in New York City was to build the Grand Hotel with Hyatt. Trump had done everything right: He'd identified the right man to speak with, he made his best pitch, and the deal was coming together. There was one thing he asked for they were not willing to give him: exclusivity. Hyatt was bigger than him, and while he was in a position to help Hyatt, he didn't have enough leverage to go making demands about New York City's broader hotel market. When he said he didn't want them opening up any new hotels next door—hotels that could compete with the one they were building with him—they balked. Why wouldn't they? Hyatt cofounder "Jay [Pritzker] is a smart guy," Trump wrote, "and he wasn't about to foreclose the future expansion of his hotel chain in one of the biggest cities in the world."

So Trump waited for a chance. And he saw one near the closing, but it wasn't a chance he had the capital to take. At the closing meeting, in a side room, Trump pointed out his worry to the bankers who held the money to finance the hotel, saying there wasn't a whole lot to stop Hyatt from opening up competition down the road. It was as obvious to the bank as it was to Trump that this wouldn't bode well for the hotel they were all going in on, so they ought to move, and they did, meeting with the Hyatt executives to let them know they weren't going to put the millions up for a hotel that didn't have exclusivity.

Now, the bank had some leverage in the "tens of millions" they were putting up. The Hyatt guys knew that, and though it probably wasn't in their best interests, they accepted.

Trump waited, got his partners where he needed them, positioned himself where he needed to be, and forced the hand.

Leverage doesn't even have to be a card you or your ally holds. Leverage can be found in the other guy's weakness, as when Trump was working to buy the future site of Trump Tower. The last piece of the puzzle was a company that owned the largest part of the property and the famous retail store inside. They were in serious financial difficulty, but with the very likely potential for more lucrative offers for the land, they were trying to worm out of the bargain they'd made to sell to Trump. Then the *New York Times* found out, printing that a deal had been reached and the building—and its store—would be sold in months. Right away, the retail store's best employees headed for the door, worried they'd lose their paychecks if they didn't secure good employment fast.

"It was becoming almost impossible to run the store," Trump recalls. "That, I believe, was the straw that broke [the company's] back. After that, they stopped balking."

The deal went through in sixty days.

"The worst thing you can possibly do in a deal is seem desperate to make it," Trump wrote. "That makes the other guy smell blood, and then you're dead. The best thing you can do is deal from strength, and leverage is the biggest strength you have. Leverage is having something the other guy wants. Or better yet, needs. Or best of all, simply can't do without."

In a free market, people make deals that benefit them

both. When you buy gas, you get what you need, but even then, someone typically comes out on top. The winners have one thing in common: They seek out and build an advantage that forces the best possible terms using anything they can, including what they have, what they're perceived to have, and what the other guy doesn't have.

Leverage is the lens through which all of Trump's decisions can be understood. Otherwise-inexplicable tweets and comments are designed with the sole purpose of creating leverage and momentum toward the deal.

In the world of politics, where deals aren't made one-on-one and players have less clear, and often less rational, motivations, this can be harder, but it still translates. It translates to every aspect of life. How can you attack Trump on the debate stage when you came to his wedding or took money from him for your campaign? Not a lot of leverage there. And indeed, some of the most hysterical parts of the primary came when different politicians were shut down over where their bread had been buttered, and Trump won those rounds handily.

Or if you're a foreign country that takes billions in American aid and benefits a great deal from American trade, what leverage do you have to stop the U.S. president from building a wall on the border? Strong promises were made, but they gained a good deal of real-world power when the United States elected him.

When it appeared that Obamacare repeal had died in

the House, Trump exerted pressure. He hit the conservative Freedom Caucus, calling them out for not voting to repeal.

"The Freedom Caucus will hurt the entire Republican agenda if they don't get on the team, & fast," he sent out. "We must fight them, & Dems in 2018!"

It looked like an attack to a lot of Washington, but all anyone had to do to figure it out was ask an old Ted Cruz for President hand if it had been an attack and you'd hear, "No, you'll know when it's an attack. That was a prodding."

Despite only minor tinkering with the bill, outside conservative groups decided it was the best deal they could get, so they held their fire, and concessions were made by members of both the Freedom Caucus and the liberal Republican Tuesday Group, which saw one of its cochairmen resign over the turmoil. The vote was passed and sent to the Senate.

The news media were quick to point out that the victory press conference Trump hosted with House members shortly after the vote was far before any real bill was on the president's desk, but the message to the Senate was clear: Pass repeal, or you will be blamed from the highest perch of the U.S. government.

You don't have to be president to have something someone else wants. It's one of the most crucial parts of any deal you can make. Bluster and courage will get you some of the way, but they can sink you if there's nothing behind it. You have to use what you have to develop this, and keep an open mind:

Resources aren't just things like timber and coal; they can come in all sorts of shapes. Use them all.

RULE 5: Use Your Resources

Donald Trump took a lot of heat during the primary. Some of it was deserved. Over the preceding few years, for example, the Republican National Committee had built up the means for a nationwide infrastructure to assist the nominee, and most party loyalists were worried that Trump and his organization were not utilizing this at all.

But what did they miss?

Trump did not pursue any of the typical models for presidential candidates. He didn't rely on a close-knit group of political veterans who advised him on his every move. He didn't even use a lot of the internal polling that most major campaigns rely on to track their actions and decisions. He did, however, do something that most folks he ran against didn't: listen to outside advice. And while the good old boys from Texas, Florida, Ohio, Chicago, or wherever else the candidate is from may be helpful in certain situations, Trump's work outside of his circle may have broadened his mind—and, secretly, his D.C. support—more than any of his competition.

Senator Jim DeMint was a good example. A staunchly conservative politician from South Carolina, DeMint had taken over the Heritage Foundation, the world's leading conservative think tank, just a few years prior. In 1980, Heritage had found a key role advising President Ronald Reagan and even providing the blueprint for his first years in office—"Mandate for Leadership." But since those days, Heritage had been effectively marginalized by a Republican leadership that paid lip service to conservative policies without executing them. When they reached out to most Republican campaigns, the word back was "Thanks, but no thanks." They had their own people for whatever policy Heritage's experts were concerned with.

Trump didn't. He didn't really know policy. He knew business, golf, entertainment, hospitality, construction, branding, travel, public relations, and, some might say, interior decoration, but not the weeds of policy. And neither did a lot of the people he'd worked with over the years. But for the past four decades, conservatives had been thinking, writing position papers, giving speeches, and generally paying an army of eggheads to do their thing. Here was a chance to put that army on the march.

Jim DeMint and Donald Trump couldn't be much different. DeMint is a quiet, understated man who rarely curses and got his hair cut by the barbers across the street from the office. Sitting next to him in a barber chair, getting my own hair cut one day, I wondered if he might be annoyed at the preachy, liberal rap song "Same Love" playing on the radio, then realized there's pretty much no chance he had any idea who "Macklemore" was or gave two hecks—he was just getting a haircut.

After they were done talking, Trump got to what he thought was the point: How much money do you want? None, DeMint told him. Heritage just wanted his ear. It might have seemed foolish to some at the time, not accepting a check from a very rich man, but it paid off: Trump respects people who demonstrate their worth instead of asking for handouts, and as his own stature grew within the Republican Party, groups like the Heritage Foundation, the conservative lawyers of the Federalist Society, and the guys at the Institute for Energy Research grew in usefulness to the campaign.

What does a New York real estate developer do when he needs to come up with a list of Supreme Court nominees that will please the right wing of a political party he's kind of new to? Trump's first whack—semijokingly suggesting his sister, who is a judge—did not go over so well. His next move was to call Heritage and Federalist Society leaders to come up with a list. They were happy to help.

And when he was elected president and needed people who understood the federal government but weren't Obama appointees, he could once again turn to helpful outside groups to staff his transition, White House, and departments.

Donald Trump didn't have the legions of political friends most politicians pick up on their ways through lower offices, and as an outsider, he didn't recruit many of D.C.'s freelance politicos, but by tapping into a network eager to push the conservative agenda, he leveraged a resource available to most but not tapped by many, and he used it to win.

Despite some well-founded rumors of how impressed he is with himself, Trump has never been too proud to get the best people on the job. He became a bona fide New York City hero in the mid-1980s when he took over the rebuilding of Wollman Rink in Central Park; the project was years behind deadlines and already had $13 million in the hole when the announcement had come that they would need to restart from scratch. Trump saw a chance and made an offer. The mayor balked, publicly releasing a cheeky letter that backfired in the press and forced him to accept the businessman's offer. Now it was time to perform—on a public deadline with the whole city watching and the guys in City Hall hoping for an embarrassment.

"Since I myself knew absolutely nothing about building rinks," Trump admitted after it was all over, "I set out to find the best skating rink builder I could."

And he had a good guess as to where to look: Canada. And from start to finish, he followed this model, getting the best people in the room and riding them hard until the job was finished. The rink was opened in time for winter.

It's easy to consider "resources" to be limited to things like money and supplies, but the resource most readily available—and useful—to men and women rich and poor is people: friends, allies, partners, colleagues, bosses, employees, husbands, wives, children, and neighbors. When you need help moving or building, making a sale or finishing a project, rising up and moving out, relationships are the best rungs of any ladder. And if you're there when they need you, the best of them will be there when you need them.

We all rely principally on ourselves, and it is often true that if you want the job done right, do it yourself. But it's a good man who realizes he isn't always the expert, and no one high or low can go it alone.

Of course, that doesn't mean you aren't your own, and you will be the number-one winner and loser for the decisions you make. It's your life, and as Trump illustrates in nearly everything he's done, you're the brand.

RULE 6: Be True to Your Brand

George Washington, Dwight D. Eisenhower, Donald Trump. Seems like a strange list, but besides serving as presidents of the United States, all three were known to practically every voter in the country before they assumed office.

The father of the country and the supreme commander of the Allied forces have quite a bit more claim to fame, but it shows the power of television, newspapers, and the brand that an entertainer and businessman is able to build over his life. Donald Trump was in the papers since he was a young man, constantly promoting, inserting, and celebrating himself.

I'm guilty of posing with a friend in the Plaza Hotel hallway where Trump told *Home Alone*'s Kevin McCallister how to find the lobby. It's fine: Hotel employees are used to tourists. And in the years since that 1992 children's movie cameo, he spent fourteen years hosting different versions of the reality game show *The Apprentice*.

Before the TV show, he'd wondered which was the best track to brand stardom—movies or television. He took advice from friends and acquaintances and settled on the medium that could put him in Americans' living rooms every evening. Even then, he was skeptical of reality TV, saying the medium was for "bottom feeders." But he was sold on the brand promotion.

"My jet's going to be in every episode," he'd go on to tell NBC's old publicity director. "The [Trump] Taj [casino] is going to be featured. Even if it doesn't get ratings, it's still going to be great for my brand."

"Trump had been famous for more than a generation," Michael Kranish and Marc Fisher write in *Trump Revealed,* "but a TV show of his own would allow him to mold his image as never before, giving Americans the chance to see him in a way they perceived as unmediated."

It was worth the few hours he'd have to spend per show.

While most top CEOs prefer to stay hidden, Trump understood from the first day he entered business that his name is his brand, and atop a sprawling, international company that represents him everywhere it goes, he has worked to cultivate that brand. Even as he's surrendered control of his company and taken hits from stores and consumers wary of the politics his name now represents, his rising stature has contributed to the rising success of his D.C. hotel, his Mar-a-Lago club, and his properties around the world.

His name was so synonymous with luxury that in 1989, two sets of decadent limousines were released under his brand by Cadillac, the brand of American GM created to focus on American luxury. And, as he's reminded the country over and over again for quite a few years, his book *The Art of the Deal* has sold more than a million copies, by some estimates. It's the art of the brand.

Some might call it shameless, and they have a point. But at the same time, it's a certain fearlessness. As with most things, it isn't embarrassing if you aren't embarrassed.

In years past, presidents and the men who wished they were have gotten themselves into trouble time and time again by breaking one old rule, summed up succinctly by President Barack Obama himself: When handed a fitted Navy football helmet in 2013, he mused between laughs, "You don't put stuff on your head if you're president. That's Politics 101. You never look good wearing something on your head."

His instincts were right. His tall, skinny frame would have looked ridiculous in a business suit and a football helmet, and the picture would bug him for years. *Politico* magazine traced the rule back to President Calvin Coolidge, who posed for a picture in an American Indian headdress despite his advisers' protests. The picture can be found under the slide show "History's Worst Political Photo Ops."

The most famous presidential photo faux-pas might be nonpresident Michael Dukakis, whose campaign had actually had a rule against hats because the candidate looked silly in them. The picture of him riding a tank with a helmet, including a name tag, would haunt the campaign's final doomed days against George H. W. Bush. "The second we saw that picture on the six o'clock news," one of his advisers recalled, "we had pains in our stomach."

Trump shattered this rule, alongside many others, donning a red American trucker hat with his campaign slogan, "Make America Great Again," wearing it proudly at a campaign speech near the Mexican border and later even handing one to Jeff Sessions, the genteel senator from Alabama, who awkwardly put it on, looked uncomfortable, and pulled it back off again.

Trump was mocked by the political and media establishments, but he sure looked comfortable, and the hats became a phenomenon, sparking twenty-five-dollar campaign donations and fistfights across the country. At 3 a.m. after Election Day, after having spent a long evening amid tears and apocalyptic wailing at Hillary's campaign headquarters, I sat at a desk in a hotel room a few floors above the crowds awaiting Trump's victory speech when I received a Facebook message from a cousin in Scotland.

"I have work in four hours but cannot switch off!" she

wrote. "Can you bring us a couple of hats next June, please? The red ones . . . Just call it a wedding gift!"

I delivered them at the end of April 2017. The happy couple threw them on and posed for a picture in a Glasgow Airport bar. "He's quite popular here," John told me.

A "Politics 101" rule broken, and an ocean bridged, by a simple brand.

He's been criticized for being boastful, tacky, and all sorts of things, but it doesn't stick because Donald Trump is Donald Trump, and he isn't embarrassed or afraid to be himself. It's difficult to think of a politician since Bill Clinton as comfortable in his own skin, and it shows. He is the brand, and it doesn't take a lot of money to do it.

Because brand is just a high-end word for reputation, and in a social media age when mortifying and shameless broadcasts are fairly common, it's necessary for the successful person to remember how important their reputation is. Yes, it's based on your character, and yes, it precedes you.

Even for young people starting out in a new city, the first thing most employers do is look them up on social media. What do the pictures say about them? Do you have any mutual friends who can speak to their character?

When you're selling yourself, writing the rules, bringing on good people, seeking leverage, and seeking others' assistance, your reputation is what you've walked in the door with first. So don't ever disregard it.

Sure, you'll make enemies. That, as Winston Churchill

says, means you've stood for something. But if it's done in the service of being yourself, and you yourself are good, you've got nothing to fear. Own it, tailor it. It's yours, so it ought to fit you well.

And you'll also make allies.

2

★

Embrace the Chaos

Chaos is never too far from our affairs.

Even when we're foolish enough to convince ourselves it is.

On October 31 in Manhattan, the *New York Post* learned that Hillary Clinton's staffers had planned a two-minute Hudson River fireworks display set to go off thirty minutes after the polls closed.

On November 7 in Pittsburgh, Hillary was photographed signing the cover of *Newsweek*'s commemorative issue, titled "Madam President." Shops across the country had already received their shipments.

On Election Night, back under the warm lights of the city, the *New York Times*' writers blithely reported that Hillary Clinton had an 85 percent chance of being elected president.

At 7:42 p.m. on November 8, *Politico*'s Playbook sent out its newsletter on "where the race stands." It told its D.C. readers about the "early snoozers" that were being called, reflected that there was "no surprise here" that McConnell will "run for GOP leader, even in minority," and gave us 171 words on the free food that reporters were being served as they wrote the last chapter of Her victorious campaign. "Politico has chicken, shrimp, veggies/sides, salads."

They had no idea how close their lives were to being turned upside down. None of them did. They'd lived far removed from anything of the sort for most of their professional lives.

While much of the world has burned at one time or another over the past 150 years, the United States has generally maintained order and a functioning civil society since the Civil War ended at Appomattox Court House. But peace in our borders doesn't mean our nature changes, and in the boardroom as in politics, chaos is closer than we'd ever like to think. And chaos holds the power to lay waste to the best-laid plans of the competition—particularly when overseen by someone capable of taking advantage of it.

When chaos strikes, whether by design or circumstance, a leader is faced with the choice of using it for their own gain or letting it consume them and their organization.

Donald Trump does all of this, capitalizing on chaos at nearly every turn. He appears to thrive on it.

In his business career, he has seen opportunities where others saw disaster. And in politics, chaos has followed wherever he goes, massively disrupting the established field, dominating the press, and foiling his opponents at every step, keeping everyone guessing and on their toes.

The whirlwind that is the Trump show truly embodies the virtuous surprise and confusion that can vex even the most formidable opponents. If you can keep your head above it, chaos can actually be a brilliant way of running an enterprise.

RULE 7: Chaos Confuses the Enemy

Donald Trump is always on the move, seemingly never content to be still. This has gotten him in trouble—trouble the newspapers have documented well over the past forty years— but it's also been integral to his success. While parts of his life, like a private plane, are a little hard to imagine in most of our hectic lives on the road, for the fast movers among us his fast-food habit sure is familiar.

It isn't just movement for movement's sake, though. Trump demands action every day. While patience is necessary in certain long-term negotiations—as when holding out for a good deal from the city and other partners when building his TV City development—once the deal starts moving, decisiveness has proven a key to Trump's success.

When fighting over the final moments of buying the land for Trump Tower, the leaks to the press (from none other than Donald Trump) caused an absolute panic in the department store he was trying to buy, as top employees turned on leaders they expected to betray them, forcing the store to bolt to the finish line just to stop hemorrhaging cash.

In this case, the sellers had begun to pull back from the

deal with Trump because they had figured out something Trump says he already knew—the land they were sitting on was worth considerably more than they were about to sell to Trump for. By forcing an already weakened party's hand, and creating that sense of chaos by setting off employee panic, Trump was able to win out in a tenuous deal.

In the final stages of a deal with Hyatt, chaos was once again Trump's friend and ally. He unleashed the bankers he had enlisted in his cause on a room of unsuspecting Hyatt executives with the hard ultimatum on no other Hyatts in New York City if they wanted the financing. Hyatt was given one hour to make its decision—the equivalent of spraying someone's face with a fire extinguisher, spinning them around, and saying "find the exit"—a feeling Donald Trump was happy to impart to his could-be partners.

"What I had going for me was that [Hyatt cofounder] Jay Pritzker wasn't at the closing," Trump wrote of the negotiations. Pritzker had balked when Trump had first floated such an arrangement, and Trump knew it. "The executive representing Hyatt tried to reach Jay, but it turned out he was in Nepal, mountain climbing, and he couldn't be reached."

Too bad.

That executive's carefully rehearsed calculus was dashed. Would he surrender a giant deal for a downtown hotel and walk away? Would he close other doors to future deals in the city? Trump was moving faster than him, forcing emissaries of the man in charge to make snap decisions of real importance while their world was in flux. "I was taking a chance, because right then and there the whole financing could have fallen through," Trump later admitted.

But it didn't. He took a chance, confounding the other players in the room, and he won. These days, we can watch YouTube montages of Trump throwing his opponents off balance. Back then, to get a front-row seat you had to have some money to lose.

And in the old days, these battles took place in the corporate world, where a top executive can make a snap decision in a largely private setting. In politics, it's a lot harder to change tracks and confront chaotic circumstances. See Exhibit A: One John Ellis "Jeb!" Bush.

When Jeb Bush declared he was ascending to the Republican nomination, a lot of Washington types figured he'd clean up. He hit all the bases his team thought were right early, scaring mean old Mitt Romney away with crows about the money they'd raise, bringing on a team of self-important blowhards known in newspapers as "veteran consultants," and running on an open, loving vision for the country supported by free trade and peppered with tax cuts and a strong military. That cheesy host with the spiked hair on the Food Channel couldn't have written a better recipe for a win.

Then along came Donald Trump, who gutted Jeb! like he was an ingredient for chowder. Trump hit him on the money he raised, saying Bush was beholden to special interests; he hit him on the team he gathered, calling them lobbyists and donors; he attacked Bush's plan on immigration to cheers from the base; and he even threw over a few tables in the GOP's temple to free trade.

And when Bush attacked back, touting the brother he thought was his secret weapon, Trump did the unthinkable in a party primary—he attacked the last Republican president's record on American security.

"I became Trump's biggest fan," wrote J. D. Vance, a former Marine and the author of *Hillbilly Elegy*. "I wanted him to go for the jugular. I wanted him to inquire whom, precisely, George W. Bush had kept safe. Was it the veterans lingering in a bureaucratic quagmire at the Department of Veterans Affairs or the victims of 9/11? Was it the enlistees from my block back home, who signed their lives on the dotted line while Jeb's brother told the country to 'go shopping'—something kids like me couldn't afford to do?"

"In strategy the longest way around is often the shortest way there," British veteran and military strategist Liddell Hart wrote after living through the mindless barbarism of World War I's trenches. "A direct approach to the object exhausts the attacker and hardens the resistance by compression, whereas an indirect approach loosens the defender's hold by upsetting his balance."

He may be president now, but when Donald Trump announced his candidacy for the office, there was no clear path to victory.

The direct approach to politics, he knew, played the game his opponents played. The game they expected: get funding, secure endorsements, go out and give stump speeches, and all the rest. Their approach, played the way they would have liked, meant the winner would be the man or woman who got the most stuff.

Playing that game would have led to defeat and embarrassment for Donald Trump, so he went a different path: He gave speeches different from other politicians', he undermined his opponents constantly, he attacked anyone and everyone directly through his words and through social media, he kept his many, many foes guessing all day every day. Any other way against Jeb Bush or Hillary Clinton—lofty speeches, safe ads, TV surrogates—would have been the political equivalent of David challenging Goliath to a sword fight. This way, Trump certainly wasn't guaranteed the presidency, but victory was possible.

Hart had learned about playing the opponent's game in a terrible way, climbing out of the miserable trenches to charge enemy machine-gun emplacements across open, wired fields. An entire European generation had been lost in this senselessness, and he was determined to see that Britain's young men didn't face it again. But it was an ancient idea.

"In all fighting, the direct method may be used for joining battle, but indirect methods will be needed in order to secure victory," Chinese general Sun Tzu wrote more than two thousand years before the guns of August.

Hart's indirect approach never meant not confronting the enemy—it meant hitting them hardest where they're weakest and not engaging where the enemy rules the roost.

Avoid their front lines and hit where it isn't expected. It didn't just save Trump a bitter political battle he wasn't prepared to win; it kept his opponents unbalanced while he called the shots.

Trump flipped every Republican norm on its head, and Bush had no way to respond. He floundered, growing publicly depressed and clearly perplexed as to what the heck was going on.

"If Jeb Bush hadn't run for president, Donald Trump would have had to invent him," read a column in the *Atlantic*. "The former Florida governor was Trump's perfect foil."

Republicans found themselves unable to predict what Trump would do next, which was "highly abnormal" in the kind of way your most prissy high school teacher would mutter it.

What was Rand Paul going to do next? He was going to go on about liberty and war being bad. Lindsey Graham? Free trade and war being good. Marco Rubio? The American experience and security. Chris Christie? Getting tough and talking straight. Ted Cruz? The Constitution and Obamacare. Jeb Bush? About as predictable as it gets. Bobby Jindal? Who cares.

But Trump was a loose cannon. The perfect "madman." And because of his unpredictability, his volatility, and the viciousness of his attacks, some major potential opponents like Cruz steered clear until, maybe, it was too late and Trump had grown too powerful.

The "madman" theory isn't new to the modern GOP, nor is it new to ruling in difficult times.

"At times it is a very wise thing to simulate madness," Niccolò Machiavelli, an Italian Renaissance political philosopher, wrote five hundred years ago. When those words were published, Machiavelli was already gone, and the man he wrote of, Junius Brutus, had been gone two thousand years. Five centuries after it was published, it stands true.

The madman is "less observed," Machiavelli mused, and so would "have greater opportunity to attack the Kings, and liberate his country whenever he should be given the occasion."

The "simulation" of madness, he wrote, is what allowed Brutus close enough to Caesar to end his reign.

Brutus attacked under a military emperor, and Machiavelli wrote in a dangerous court. We like to think ourselves far removed from the deadly chaos and dreadful uncertainty they faced every day, but we simply aren't.

In modern American power, Richard Nixon deployed the "madman" theory to frighten the Soviets, the Chinese Communists, and the enemy in Vietnam into thinking he was so crazy he'd do anything—the opposite of President Dwight Eisenhower, the measured statesman during the Korean War.

"I call it the Madman Theory, Bob," Nixon's chief of staff, H. R. "Bob" Haldeman, says Nixon told him. "I want the North Vietnamese to believe I've reached the point where I might do anything to stop the war. We'll just slip the word to them that, 'For God's sake, you know Nixon is obsessed about communism. We can't restrain him when he's angry—and he has his hand on the nuclear button' and Ho Chi Minh himself will be in Paris in two days, begging for peace."

"We're totally predictable," Trump told the *Washington Post* in March. "And predictable is bad. Sitting at a meeting like this and explaining my views and if I do become president, I have these views that are down for the other side to look at, you know. I hate being so open."

A few weeks later, when asked on Fox if he'd be willing to use nuclear weapons in Europe, he replied, "Europe is a big place, I'm not going to take cards off the table."

"I have a plan," he said in a September forum, "but . . . if I win, I don't want to broadcast to the enemy exactly what my plan is."

That air of unpredictability was a quality in Donald Trump that caused a lot of campaigns that might have hurt him early to hold off. Those campaigns assumed that Trump, like Claudius, was not a serious man capable of taking the crown from them. Like hobos asleep on the tracks, they didn't see him bearing down with the force of a freight train until it was far too late.

There's not a lot of evidence that the hysterical reporters

and never-Trumpers are very smart at all, and if there is, it's shrouded in so much arrogance it came to naught. Trump was consistently leading in opinion polls starting in July 2015, yet the whole way into the 2016 campaigns, most journalists, pundits, and politicians simply assumed he'd collapse at the primaries, and so lifted nary a finger to try to bring him down.

Evan McMullin, a finger-sniffing type who makes people uncomfortable, didn't even launch his "presidential campaign" to derail Trump until August of the next year. The weekend he launched it, the brain behind the idea, neoconservative Bill Kristol, spent the weekend taking the family to a theme park instead of raising money or rallying support. And when, predictably, no one cared McMullin was running for president to save the right from Trump, he named a person named Mindy Finn to be his running mate.

Mindy might truly be a nice person, but shortly after the name was announced, I was sitting at a table with Tucker Carlson and a few other *Daily Caller* editors, wondering, "Who the heck is Mindy Finn? Have you ever heard of her?"

Apparently refusing to believe Trump was sailing for the nomination, the conservatives backing last-man-standing Ted Cruz even plotted to defeat him through a rules game at the convention. To put that in perspective, in modern politics winning at the convention is the equivalent of a Kentucky Derby horse waiting to pull ahead and win the race when the competition is already holding the trophy in the Winner's Circle. But it was difficult to tell folks that. Imagine how your nerdiest childhood friend acted when excited about something—fiendish. That's what it was like to hear these guys in the cable news greenrooms, whispering that they had figured out how to beat Trump—"We're going to take it from him!"

None of it worked, of course. Ted Cruz was booed off-stage for saying "vote your conscience" instead of endorsing Trump—a move he presented as principled, but which he, incredibly, expected a rousing applause for. And when the election was over, the word is Bill Kristol was told to step aside at the magazine he'd run for more than twenty years. If he wasn't going to be profitable, his major backer reportedly reasoned, he'd better at least be influential, and in 2016, he was neither.

It was all too late in the day. They'd woken up late, missed any chance they might have had, and didn't even realize it. And once it really was late in the day, Trump's air of unpredictability was something his opponents feared the most—because they could defend against it least.

It's important to see what happened here—what Trump did, and how his opponents failed to handle it—and to internalize it. But that isn't because it can be emulated so easily as getting good people on your side or leveraging your assets.

Acting mad might help keep Caligula off your back while you write a history book in the tower, and it might even scare Ho Chi Minh, but it won't go over well with your family or your boss. What you can turn to your advantage is decisiveness in action combined with an unpredictability that keeps your opponents and potential partners guessing.

Predictability is a good characteristic in a worker bee. It can pay the bills, but it won't take you far beyond middle management. When you're working to undermine or out-maneuver a competitor, their inability to predict your next move is suddenly the kind of asset that keeps you moving up in sales or promotion or any number of aspects of competition we find ourselves wading through in the modern workplace.

With short timelines, split-second decisions, and unforeseen negotiation tactics, you can keep someone on their heels, deciding the game they're reacting to instead of allowing them to decide your day and your next move. It can be used to establish who's in command, not simply in other firms, but even in your own.

RULE 8: A Sense of Crisis Creates Demand for Command

When you stop to investigate the environments he does best in—the situations he thrives in—it's no surprise that Donald Trump, who had been publicly mulling a run for president since the late 1980s, saw the biggest win of his life in 2016.

The terror attacks and economic collapse of the 2000s shook the United States to the core, but the national adrenaline rush we experienced helped hide the severity of some of the cracks in the first decade, pushing them back a number of years. By 2010, large swaths of the South and Midwest had woken up to the sorry state of their economies and the looming fact that their government was determined to continue on the same path.

Since the new Silent Majority's tea-party uprising took place during President Obama's time in the White House, and since the passage of Obamacare really pushed it to a boil, Republicans reinstalled in the House and the Senate saw the whole situation as a vindication of their old ideas. As Jeb! and the rest of them found out, the real situation was far out of their control. For Nancy Pelosi, Harry Reid, Mitch McConnell, John Boehner, and, now, Paul Ryan, it was chaos. For Donald Trump, it was opportunity.

It wasn't the first time he'd seen an opportunity where government leaders were in a mess of their own creation. The only reason he was ever in the position to bring a Canadian ice company into New York to fix Wollman Rink was because of a time just like that.

The rink had been closed for rebuilding in 1980, and on May 22, 1986, Trump saw a *New York Times* article saying the city had to start over on construction. Two years earlier, Trump, who could see the rink from his office, had offered to take over construction for the city and had been rebuffed. This time, he sent a private letter to Mayor Ed Koch, a lifelong leftist he already had a piss-poor relationship with. In the letter, he offered to get the rink running in time for that coming winter, and then to "lease the rink from the city at a fair market rental, and run it properly after its completion."

Ed Koch, like a lot of people in political power, miscalculated his popularity versus the billionaire real estate guy's, so he wrote a public response dismissing Trump. The city's newspapers erupted at the incompetence of the city government, thundering to give the man in Trump Tower a shot.

A degree of chaos is fairly constant in life, but when it gets so bad we all start to notice, there's an opportunity. If the guy who's supposed to be in charge doesn't notice, that—that, right there—is the opportunity.

In 2010, the leaders of both parties didn't see it. They were in crisis. And while a lot of people don't care much for Rahm Emanuel, the man was on point when he admitted, "You never want a serious crisis to go to waste."

By 2016, people were mad as hell. As the primary season kicked into gear, a lot of conservatives bet that Americans were sick of the Democrat agenda, which had hit them everywhere from their pockets to their bakeries, in their doctors' offices and bathrooms. The primaries and election would show Republicans that Americans were sick of a whole lot more than just Democrats, but at the time, watchers were surprised to find out that all over the vast expanses of America that exist beyond Washington, voters were in between two very different New Yorkers.

Born in Brooklyn five years before Donald Trump entered the world, Bernie Sanders cut a very different path in life.

Political at a young age, in his twenties he moved to Vermont to get in touch with country living, distinguishing himself little before being kicked out of a hippie commune in '71 for—prophetically—talking about politics instead of working. Seriously.

Nine years later, Sanders finally landed a steady job as the socialist mayor of Burlington. A decade later, he went to Washington as a congressman. Then, in 2006, he went to Washington as a U.S. senator. Finally, in 2016, he barnstormed the country as America's first major openly socialist candidate for president in decades.

Sanders didn't build a real estate empire, international business, or TV series, and, a politician for much of his life, he didn't represent any of America's conservative spirit. In fact, the only business his wife ever ran, Burlington College, went completely under—so much so the FBI is asking questions. Sad!

Still, when the Brooklyn-accented socialist with a grandfatherly appearance hollered at the ramparts and dared to challenge Hillary Clinton and the entire political establishment, he struck a chord with people from all ages and backgrounds who were sick of what had become normal in the country.

For the second time in her would-be presidential career, Hillary Clinton didn't take the competition seriously until he was already beating her in states she'd expected to sweep. She was likely saved a second primary defeat only by Sanders's unwillingness to attack until late in the campaign and the strength of the party elite in her favor. He saw the crisis, but did not show the will to take advantage of it, and it went to waste.

Sanders thrived on the same vein of American unrest as Trump—that visceral distaste for Washington norms, lit up with rage at political parties that were completely detached from the needs of their bases.

But like he had his entire life, Donald took a different tack from Bernie's. Surveying the chaos around him, he started hitting the big guys hard and fast. When they struck back, he stood his ground, never apologizing and always pushing on.

The Trump lawyers who fought the courts over his immigration orders may have later regretted some of the bombast of his frequent statements, but with speeches, rallies, branding, and attacks, he quickly established not only that he was serious, but that he was determined to win.

The second, less-quoted part of Rahm Emanuel's famous line on crisis, explains, "And what I mean by that is it's an opportunity to do things that you think you could not do before."

Sanders did not seize it; Trump did. And only one of them is president today.

A lot of us remember watching the looting and fires during the Baltimore riots, or any of the other dozen disturbances across American cities in 2016. Crisis creates freedom to maneuver in ways people simply can't when things are better ordered. When the rules break down, well, the rules break down. And suddenly, things that appeared impossible just a few short weeks before are imminently doable.

During Obama's eight years, political correctness advanced like it was invincible. Schools were cracking down on free speech (and still are), and the White House was issuing videos instructing young people on how to speak about politics to their older (liberal translation: bigoted) relatives at family gatherings. Politicians and media figures were quick to call people with center-right viewpoints racist, and terms like "It is [insert the current year], people" were all the vogue, as if stating the year made them right and you wrong. "You're on the wrong side of history" was another casual insult with serious implications.

Mitt Romney wrote an entire book called *No Apology,* yet he apologized what seemed like every minute. But this culture of shame was unsustainable, and as Americans felt themselves censored at their own dining room tables, they rebelled. Political correctness reached a point of absurdity, and a sense of alarm began to spread.

"I'm not a politician, thank goodness," Trump told conservatives gathered in February 2015 while floating a possible run for president. "Politicians are all talk, no action. . . . I'm the only Republican that is going to say this. We've got to make this country rich again."

It's difficult to know if Trump broke the first window in the riot, or if he just identified that the windows were broken, but to the elites in D.C., New York, Los Angeles, and San Francisco, it sounded like the world was coming down.

"All change creates winners and losers in an organization," *Fortune* magazine's Geoffrey Colvin wrote in 2006, "and the caveman part of our brains is still wired to defend against loss above all. So people almost always resist change."

And of course they would. Almost no one in the media or Hollywood joined in. There was little shot that a sizable number of politicians, who rarely lead and frequently follow, would join. Tucker Carlson, then the *Daily Caller* editor in chief and a Fox morning host, wrote one of the first articles in his defense, titled "Donald Trump Is Shocking, Vulgar and Right."

"He's not just a reformer; like most effective populists," Tucker wrote, "he's a whistleblower, a traitor to his class. Before he became the most ferocious enemy American business had ever known, Teddy Roosevelt was a rich guy. His privilege wasn't incidental; it was key to his appeal. Anyone can peer through the window in envy. It takes a real man to throw furniture through it from the inside."

"The rural folk with the Trump signs in their yards say their way of life is dying, and you smirk and say what they *really* mean is that blacks and gays are finally getting equal rights and they hate it," David Wong, a liberal from a rural red state, wrote in an attempt to explain what had happened to his city friends. "But I'm telling you, they say their way of life is dying *because their way of life is dying*. It's not their imagination. No movie about the future portrays it as being full of traditional families, hunters, and coal mines. Well, except for *Hunger Games,* and that was depicted as an apocalypse.

"So yes, they vote for the guy promising to put things back the way they were, the guy who'd be a wake-up call to the blue [Democrat] islands," Wong continued on Cracked.com. "They voted for the brick through the window."

Donald Trump brought a sense of urgency as well as the leadership Tucker and Wong write of, while his opponents in both parties remained hopelessly stuck in an election mindset just four years old but already hopelessly out of date.

As the end neared, Marco Rubio, for one, tried the new rules Trump had set, but it was too late and the dirty jokes he made fell flat. Trump had emerged in the midst of a crisis, whipped it up further, taken control, and declared a new game with new rules. His opponents in the GOP were looking the wrong way when they crossed the street and were hit hard.

The Democrats in the general election, meanwhile, could only hope enough of the old rules still stood to keep him at bay, like they had with Sanders. They weren't.

In history, chaos is common and times of order are surprisingly rare, but when you're going to work at 7 and checking out at 5 to pick up the groceries, it might not seem that way.

It won't look like chaos—like people rioting and windows broken and panic. It will probably look more like change, or things might be described as "in flux." An internal crisis, maybe, when your company needs someone to step into the breach. It can make us feel awkward to step forward and say, "I'm your man," but it's essential.

"People who don't take risks," the famous business management writer Peter Drucker opined, "generally make about two big mistakes a year. People who do take risks generally make about two big mistakes a year."

Of course, life is easier when the disorder isn't in your house, but in your neighbor's—when your competition is behind in productivity or in some kind of strife.

We want to keep chaos at bay because it causes a panic in us, and one that we sometimes can't overcome long enough to take advantage of the situation. To use this sense of alarm to get things done, we need to identify it and—importantly— keep our own heads.

The easier task by far is identifying chaos in others. You get an idea when your competition's firm is in disarray; when they don't understand what the customer wants; when they don't even know what they're doing. That kind of chaos is easy.

Encouraging the chaos of open competition close to you is much more difficult (and not an advisable tactic to use in raising your children unless you want to live some real-life Greek tragedy). The key to using this in your professional life, as Trump shows, is maintaining a strict sense of your own command. Different employees might not think they need each other, but it's when they think they don't need you that your plans can come apart. Competition pushes us all to accomplish our best, and it will do the same for the people working for you when the rules—old or new—are set clearly by the boss.

Spreading chaos among competing clients is somewhere in between. As with Trump's dealings with Hyatt and the bank, so with our dealings with partners and clients: Pushed too far, a company can balk, leaving you at square one, or maybe even further back than that. If you don't maintain constant control over the leverage—what they need—you can lose it all. Money and time already spent on something are huge motivators to finish a project, and can count for a lot.

War is the ultimate in chaos. Even on a good day, everything can go wrong. As an acronym popular with the troops goes, "SNAFU: Situation normal, all f----d up."

The U.S. military's greatest thinkers spend their days predicting the next organized chaos we call war. The soldiers and officers they lead, however, often spend those same years preparing for the last war they fought, before painfully struggling toward the new way once they are already under fire. After all, those thinkers can think all they want, but it often takes a sense of alarm and urgency to get important things done. New things happening on the ground will call for new actions, new rule of engagement, and new approaches. Moreover, for too many of us, the majority of our energy goes toward preserving the old.

"If you want something new," Drucker tells us, "you have to stop doing something old."

Donald Trump wanted something new. A large number of his voters—Republicans and Democrats, conservatives and populists—wanted something new, and he brought it. Large parts of the America he and Sanders spoke to are stuck in the old, and are straining under the pressure. The chance to do something in a way your colleagues haven't, to show your customers something they hadn't considered, to flank your competition with a method they haven't employed, can lead to incredible success.

Even with hindsight, we don't know if Trump broke the first window in the riot or if he simply identified the windows that were left broken. So throw some rocks.

You have to adapt to get ahead. Politicians call it elections. Charles Darwin called it survival. But it's worth starting with something a little more manageable than the theory of evolution.

We call it competition.

RULE 9: Excellence Through Competition

Donald Trump's campaign started small. The consultants and Republican veterans wanted nothing to do with him, and the younger set that are just hungry to be on the presidential trail weren't quick to sign up: He'd toyed with running before only to decide to sit it out, and there wasn't much of an organization to enlist with.

That doesn't mean his campaign was short on personalities. Roger Stone was one. Effectively exiled from Washington Republican politics over a particularly salacious swinger scandal, Stone would later reflect, "I was like a jockey looking for a horse. You can't win the race if you don't have a horse!"

In Donald Trump, he saw a winner, and for decades he pushed the businessman closer and closer toward politics.

"The first time I laid eyes on Roger Stone he was standing poolside at a press conference on the roof of the Hotel L'Ermitage in Beverly Hills," writes Matt Labash, one of the last men in journalism to make a good living writing fascinating profiles, hating technology, and drinking whiskey like a monk. "With a horseshoe pinkie ring refracting rays from the California sun and a gangster chalk-stripe suit that looked like it had been exhumed from the crypt of Frank Costello, Stone was there to help his friend and longtime client Donald Trump explore a Reform party presidential candidacy in 2000."

Corey Lewandowski was another early campaign fixture, having met Trump at a conservative New Hampshire conference in 2014. Lewandowski told Trump he was the best there was, and Trump liked it. Stone, a man obsessed with winning at any cost and sporting a tattoo of Richard Nixon on his back, disagreed with Corey's assessment of himself. But for Trump, that was just fine.

The night before the Republican convention kicked off, I joined Tucker Carlson, Matt Labash, CBS's Will Rahn, *Fox*

& Friends host Clayton Morris, WWE-wrestler-styled conspiracy theorist Alex Jones, an NPR reporter, and, of course, Roger Stone for a boozy dinner at Cleveland's Luca Italian Cuisine.

Alex Jones helped himself to Will Rahn's meatballs, which he insisted Labash try, while Labash protested that whiskey was all he needed. "Here comes the airplane!" Jones yelled, while buzzing the fork into Labash's mouth. "This," Labash promised, "is going in the profile."

To the side, Stone, who was no longer even on the Trump campaign, earnestly laid out the case that Bill Clinton is a rapist and Donald Trump is the savior of America. He and Jones, the loyal soldier promised, would be causing a raucous bit of ruckus that week, and Trump would be elected president that fall. He didn't disappoint.

"You're a sick dude, Roger Stone," I heard a sweaty guy with an Internet show screaming two days later. "You're a sick man, Roger Stone!"

Jones and Stone had wandered onto Cenk Uygur's set in the convention media hall, hijacking the show and setting off a screaming match that has since earned millions of YouTube views.

"First of all, Alex, this ain't your f---ing show, and Roger, it surely ain't your f---ing show!" Cenk screamed as I walked up and security came down. Roger Stone loves the spotlight—and he's not a good sharer.

Almost from the start, the Trump campaign began jockeying and infighting, with people taking sides and sniping at each other incessantly through leaks to the press and whispers to the boss. In the hull of a campaign designed to win the greatest competition on earth—the U.S. presidency— a fierce competition was taking place.

Stone was an early loser. Despite years of loyal service, he quit (or was fired, which Trump says is the case) shortly after one of his last remaining allies, Sam Nunberg, was fired over racist Facebook posts (rumored to have been leaked by Lewandowski, who denies it). Stone had been left behind, and Lewandowski became the new fixture, perpetually lurking by the boss's side.

"A campaign manager should be at headquarters counting up points and plotting the course with the staff," one veteran campaign operative told me at an early morning Holiday Inn breakfast on the campaign trail. "Corey clearly isn't doing that—he's always at events, always standing by his boss's side. How can he be managing the campaign if he's out here?"

Someone who'd known Trump for years interjected: "He needs to be next to Trump. If you aren't talking to him at that moment, he's not listening. Proximity is the key to the power."

But people on the campaign also knew they needed some experience in the room, and Paul Manafort, a veteran political wrangler who'd helped President Gerald Ford fend off Ronald Reagan's primary challenge at the 1976 convention, was brought on. The word was he was the best at internal convention infighting. Lewandowski, a man who had BS'd his way from New Hampshire cop to the head of a presidential campaign, disagreed with the campaign's assessment of Paul. But for Trump, that was just fine.

Donald Trump had known Paul since the 1980s, when he was a partner in Black, Manafort, [Roger] Stone & Kelly. They were among the first to work on Reagan's 1980 campaign, kept busy representing Trump, and rarely met a dictator they wouldn't work with. Unfortunately for Trump, those connections with suspicious Russians and Ukrainians would lead to months of trouble when Democrats scrambled to explain how Clinton was defeated.

And the next to hit the road was Lewandowski, walked out of Trump Tower by security after a long and public newspaper feud ended with a brief morning meeting where even his allies had stayed mum.

Manafort pulled the campaign through the convention, working with allies to fend off a potential coup from conservatives unhappy with Trump's nomination, but in the high-pressure, cutthroat environment Trump demanded, even his old battleship couldn't stay afloat.

"Paul Manafort, a professional Republican political operative since the 1970s, was supposed to impose order on Donald J. Trump's chaotic presidential campaign," his political obituary in the *New York Times* began. "On Friday, the chaos devoured him."

Their giddiness shined through. The folks in New York City who've never built anything bigger than a feature story looked at this move as yet another sign Trump would never win.

Trump isn't simply competitive, he feeds on competition. The best, the biggest, the shiniest; buildings, courses, even—and this has gotten him in trouble—girls. It's the life he leads, the standard he holds himself to, and the bar that he expects his employees to meet.

And if you're working for him, you're living in his world. If you do a Google search for Donald Trump campaign infighting, you'll find hundreds of newspaper articles spanning the eighteen months of the campaign. It's an interesting exercise, with anonymous quotes about the allegedly doomed campaign mixed in with clear scorn from reporters who didn't think he had a chance.

As figures popped up and were cut down, and as the campaign barreled toward eventual victory, the stakes continued to rise. Running a campaign was one thing. How about now running the most powerful country in the world?

"The drama is worse than what you read," veteran political reporter Mike Allen wrote at the end of March 2017. That was pretty difficult to imagine, but it had been said before. And before, through thick and thin, win and loss, Trump's star had continued to rise.

By the time he was elected president, two sides of his campaign team had publicly formed: the populist rabble-rousers, and the established professional Republicans. (The conservatives, meanwhile, stayed quiet and burrowed deep.)

The populists were strong in his administration and had the vote behind them, but were weak in Washington outside of news outlets and activist groups, which are not so well organized. The professional Republicans were weaker inside his administration, maybe because of slow and hesitant support for his candidacy, but they have the ear of his family and they have large power structures built in the city he was coming to. Both were important to govern. And by all appearances, Trump decided to pit them against each other, just as he had pit Stone, Lewandowski, and Manafort against each other on the campaign trail.

Right away, he named to top advisory posts men who were loyal to him and also leaders in those two camps—Steve Bannon, the populist bomb-thrower, and Reince Priebus, the professional Republican.

Bannon and Priebus went to great lengths to appear as friends in public, but even if that was true—and it likely wasn't—the camps they represented certainly didn't like each other, and reporters and leakers near and far from the White House managed to whip up a lot of drama between them. It was a risk, and the chaos it came from could create more, but at that time Trump needed both the guys whose ideas earned the votes he had required to win and the guys who have the institutional knowledge to pass them into law.

It may appear to be chaos from the outside, and for the people in charge of staffing the administration it certainly was. But to Trump, he had two leaders he wanted, both fiercely loyal to him and determined for him to succeed even while holding starkly different positions on what success looks like.

"I am thrilled to have my very successful team continue with me in leading our country," Trump said at the time. "Steve and Reince are highly qualified leaders who worked well together on our campaign and led us to a historic victory. Now I will have them both with me in the White House as we work to make America great again."

And time and time again, the media was frustrated when Trump dashed the narratives they'd built up and convinced themselves of. Narratives like "this person is about to be fired," or "this person is in charge," or "this person is on the outs."

While Trump shows no hesitation to sack people who need to go, five months into the administration, the populist Stephen Bannon, the man the media had marked for dead months prior, earned a major victory with the United States' withdrawal from the Paris Agreement. There had been a competition, no doubt, with pro-Agreement White House forces like Ivanka Trump and Jared Kushner bringing experts and world leaders before Trump in an effort to save the accord, but while the competition played out, Trump made his call.

And by the time people started to actually lose their jobs,

the guessing had gone on so long that no reporters were even able to brag about it, and Wolf Blitzer was seen on air lecturing CNN's chief political analyst on good versus bad sources.

Trump's love for competition doesn't end with staffing. A much safer place to deploy competition is outside the organization, and weeks after Trump had begun appointing his senior staff, he brought his theories of the competition chaos breeds to the country's financial dealings, tackling government contracting—a place not used to top-level shake-ups.

In December, Trump met with the heads of Boeing and Lockheed Martin, two major aerospace companies with giant contracts with the United States military. He told Boeing he wanted to end cost overflows on their Air Force One project. After the meeting, the *Washington Times* reported, "the meeting with Boeing seemed to go better," and that the CEO told reporters, "We're going to get it done for less than that, and we're committed to working together to make sure that happens."

"The Lockheed CEO," the *Times* continued, "refused to speak to reporters, and Mr. Trump said they were engaged in a 'dance' over the costs."

The very next day, Lockheed's long-term spending layouts for its very pricey F-35 project took another step toward chaos when Trump tweeted, "Based on the tremendous cost and cost overruns of the Lockheed Martin F-35, I have asked Boeing to price-out a comparable F-18 Super Hornet!"

This was not the kind of negotiating that companies of

this size, working on projects of this magnitude, are used to. Of course, a bunch of reporters—reporters who'd never sold a thing or found a government spending program that should be cut—lost their minds. Trump was doing things way differently than anyone was used to, and he was creating chaos.

The tension rose even further in January, when the president took calls from Lockheed's CEO and the Air Force's project overseer while Boeing's CEO was in the room.

"After weeks of pressure from President Trump," the *New York Times* reported early the following month, "Lockheed Martin agreed on Friday to a somewhat larger price cut on its F-35 fighters than it had on the last few orders, and finally brought the cost of the main version below $100 million for each jet."

Once again, his legions of critics hopped about attacking the president, stating with confidence in papers across the country that the drop in price was predicted before and had nothing to do with Donald Trump. That is until a reporter actually asked Lockheed's CEO if Trump's unorthodox style of Oval Office negotiating had an effect. "Absolutely," she said.

It appeared to a large number of Trump's harshest critics that the administration was bumbling through the presidency, committing faux pas and heaping insults on the Pentagon's closest business partners. In the real world outside of the D.C. and New York snow globes, the new president had clear wins for the taxpayer. We're getting bad deals, Trump had told American voters as he ran for office. He would renegotiate those deals, he promised. America would win again.

Trump created competition by identifying weaknesses and exploiting them to instigate a sense of unease. Don't be comfortable, he told both staff and competitors. Don't relax even for a second. You may have the job, you may have the contract, but that does not mean you will keep it. There are jobs some of us have held where you can just mail it in. Sometimes you will rise without much effort; often you can just coast along. That stillness is the enemy of productivity. Trump demands movement. And whether coming to work to produce or leaving work to vote, Trump, like a lot of good leaders, knows that unease is the key to motion.

The high stakes show the holes Trump exploited on the campaign trail, in the White House, and in his governance more clearly in hindsight than they may have appeared at the time. Without doubt, they're more clear than the spaces for competition and unease right in front of us in our own lives.

Identifying opportunity is one of the most difficult aspects of a successful life. There's a long list of country songs filled with Woulda, Coulda, and Shoulda. The first opportunities—and the easiest ones to seize—can come along when you're young and have less to lose. Fewer responsibilities, fewer consequences. And true enough, when all you have to worry about is your rent, food, and beer budget, you're best situated to take the risks you are more careful about when you have a family to feed and a mortgage to pay.

Don't spend those years waiting. Less freedom to take risks doesn't mean there are declining chances to pursue something more than today's paycheck. The extra work because the boss is out, the better deal when the market is down, the piece of property in a rough neighborhood, the investment when your buddies are skittish.

Because of life's general hecticness, many of the best opportunities are unforeseen. If they were easy to spot, they wouldn't be a special chance anyhow. Surprise can be an adversary in this world. But in a hard competition, surprise can also be your best friend.

RULE 10: Chaos Communication Theory

Chaos can be a terrible enemy, paralyzing decision-making abilities and causing a panic. Alternatively, it can be a great friend, creating opportunities where before there was simply the way things were. Finally, it can be a weapon used to keep opponents on their heels, unable to gain any ground because they're constantly reacting.

For Donald Trump, it was all of these things. And for his opponents, it was a nightmare.

In modern politics, messages are carefully crafted in focus groups and all other imaginable types of tests. After that, they're practiced, refined, and repeated. Life covering politics on the road sounds like a fun time, and sure, there's lots of fun to be had. But there's also the grind inherent in driving from gymnasium to backyard, auditorium to front yard, hearing the smooth senator with the sharp haircut and the carefully unbuttoned "casual" collared shirt, neatly pressed.

There's a reasoning behind it. The whole point of traveling through the countryside is pressing new hands the same way and telling new people the same message. But in a national campaign, where almost every stop I hit had Fox News's Carl Cameron standing in front of the camera waiting for the candidate to say something worth calling home about, it doesn't give him much to talk about.

Imagine reporting back, "Carly Fiorina promised this afternoon to simplify the tax code, an oath she hasn't made on the trail since two hours ago, 73 miles away, in a similar-looking building to a slightly different audience." The only thing that rivals TV reporters' ability to make it seem interesting is guys like "Campaign Carl's" ability to maintain focus, talking straight into a camera without a script while voters hoot and holler inches from his head. It's impressive.

And so was Trump's ability to make news. Because he didn't follow all that politics. Heck, he didn't even take polls (no polls was probably not his best move, but it worked). Trump made news because Trump used surprise on a daily basis. A large part of it was not having a script, relying on his gut and the mood of the room to guide the speeches reporters frequently criticized as "rambling" even while they aired them in their entirety.

"Most people are surprised by the way I work," he wrote in the late 1980s. "I play it very loose. I don't carry a briefcase.

It might not have worked for, say, Mitt Romney, another immensely successful businessman, though one with a very different style of work and politics. But it did for Trump.

"You can't be too imaginative or entrepreneurial if you've got too much structure," he continued. "I prefer to come to work each day and just see what develops."

And much to the frustration of his opponents, so did the whole world. For a decade, pundits have predicted the end of television, but 2016 was the most interesting thing we've seen on TV since the Gulf War first brought live chaos safely into our living rooms. America was glued to the set like a twelve-month white Ford Bronco chase, and months after the inauguration, we remain glued to the set in record numbers.

"It's impossible," a consultant on the Marco Rubio for President campaign confided to me one evening while we waited for the debate to come on. "They air everything this guy says, and it's garbage! We put out a real policy—and one, by the way, that actually has a chance of winning an election—and nothing."

Maybe, I suggested, say something that's both interesting and new? He chuckled, and we had a drink.

He was annoyed—beyond annoyed, really—and it was

understandable. He had a young and handsome candidate who looked good on TV, had an inspirational story and all the talking points a quarter century of Republican elections suggested were necessary, but couldn't penetrate the noise created by Donald Trump.

"[Newt Gingrich] calls it noise," Brian Phillips, a straight-shooting conservative communications operative on the Cruz for President campaign, told me after the election was over. "Sometimes noise is good even amongst Republicans fighting Republicans. Sometimes the noise will drown out the left's ability, or your opposition's ability, to get any message out.

"Even though it may not necessarily be the thing you want to talk about that day, that noise helps you strategically because they're talking about what you're talking about. And Trump was an absolute master at it."

And the "noise" Donald Trump created didn't simply take the oxygen out of the room and drown out his opponents; it dictated what their day would be spent on.

"That became a real issue in our campaign, because I worked on the communications side, and whether it was strategic on their part or whether it was just sort of cultural because that's who Trump was, every day we were in the middle of having our six thirty, seven o'clock call talking about what we're talking about that day, Fox News and CNN are already—he's already driving the news that day," Phillips explained.

"We would literally be in the middle of talking about what we we're going to say that day and which reporters we were going to call and that kind of thing, and it wouldn't matter. They'd be like, 'Oh, I love your [news story] pitch, but what do you think about what Trump said today?'"

Before long, campaigns staffed by very capable political veterans were being scheduled by tweets sent by the opposition just after the media were waking up in the morning.

"And, again, was it strategic or was it cultural?" Phillips asked. "Was it just who he was? People can debate that, but it was very effective. And we probably learned that lesson too late in the campaign before we started to make a move to combat that. And we did, we started doing [press] gaggles in the morning, we'd do press conferences early. So we started to combat some of that. So we were nimble and able to do that, but it was certainly something that he was able to make a strategic advantage."

And it didn't end after the primaries.

In the days after the election, with the thoroughly battered Clintons in hiding and Harry Reid on his way to pasture, there wasn't a lot of noise coming from the incoming Senate minority leader, New York's Chuck Schumer. When he finally mustered his voice, it was to say that the president-elect wasn't popularly elected, which made zero difference to Schumer's sad fate. What did Trump respond with? Trump tweeted that he liked Schumer and he was smart. In response, the Democrat found himself in the strange position of denying this.

"He was not my friend," Schumer moaned.

By January 4, the Democrats were finally ready to unveil their big new opposition motto: "Make America Sick Again." If any of your friends remember that one, give them a dollar.

By the end of the same month, Trump was making fun of Schumer for crying at a press conference.

"He doesn't even know me!" Chuck protested.

Over the past decade, inability to penetrate the political noise has been largely a Republican problem, while Democrats have hewn to disciplined messaging. Trump changed that, though not with any messaging discipline of his own—simply through throwing curves, strikes, and balls so quickly, Chuck's neck hurt keeping up.

The opposition can't have a message, because they don't know where Trump is going tomorrow. What are they going to do when they're boxed in by political "rules" Trump won't follow?

The strategy looks like throwing a hundred messages and seeing which ones stick. Evil rich guy? Russian agent? Secret racist? Woman hater? Anti-Semite? Old and unstable? Literal Hitler? Chain-gun-toting Mecha-Hitler?

All of the above?

Throwing out insults or changing the subject isn't going to work for too long at home or in the workplace. But those are just tactics—parts of Trump's broader strategy. The keys to the larger plan are to not let yourself become predictable, to decide for yourself what you're working on and communicating, and, if you're good at it, to decide for yourself what the people around you are working on and communicating.

Predictability can be a good characteristic in a worker, but not in a leader. Not to confuse predictability with dependability—it's necessary to be dependable; for your colleagues and partners to "predict" with confidence that you will be early to work, that you'll get the job done, that you will deliver the best product.

Predictability is something else. The dictionary defines it as "behaving or occurring in a way that is expected." You don't want your moves to be simply expected. You don't want people to already know what you're going to do before you do it. They won't respect it if they like you, and if they don't like you, they'll use it against you.

The worst is if the people and firms you're competing against know what you're going to do at a given moment. When that happens, you'll lose.

Deciding what you are working on, and what you are communicating, is the second part. It's an essential aspect of defining who you are—what your brand is. It will prove key to setting yourself apart in the eyes of your boss, colleagues, or partners, and it will play a part in the opportunities you're provided.

Against your competitors, it can allow you to decide the conversation. Pepsi doesn't talk about Coca-Cola because Pepsi wants to—they have to bring up their competitor in their commercials because the soda game is defined by Coke.

Coke sets the terms of the discussion, and all else comes around it. You can do this in your life. We're not a product like a can of soda, but just like a corporation seeking to advertise its brand, we have things that are of crucial interest to ourselves. Serve them, promote them, and keep those interests at the forefront.

That isn't to say people should brag more. Don't brag. You need to be a billionaire with a TV show to make bragging funny, and if you aren't, you just look like an ass. It's not talking about himself that put Donald Trump ahead (although he does talk about himself quite a bit)—it was his agenda that was front and center: immigration, trade, Obamacare, and winning in wars.

"Think back on the last few weeks," former Secretary of Defense Donald Rumsfeld wrote in his book *Rumsfeld's Rules*. "How much time did you spend responding to the emails that appeared in your inbox, or participating in meetings initiated by others? How much time did you spend answering incoming calls discussing somebody else's priorities?

"Without the discipline and time invested in strategic planning, one of two things is likely to happen. Your organization will be buffeted by outside events and forced to be reactive. Or it will stay on autopilot, propelled by the inertia of policies and plans that were decided months or years before.

"If you are working from your inbox"—or someone else's communication—he succinctly concluded, "you are working on other people's priorities."

If you're good enough, you can define not simply your own priorities, but those of the people around you as well.

Marco and Jeb! wanted to talk about immigration as "an act of love," but they couldn't because Donald Trump defined the terms of the conversation, framing it from the perspective of America's put-upon working poor. John Kasich wanted to talk about the wonders of free trade, but Donald Trump was louder and he was first—and he wanted to talk about how America has been getting a bum deal for decades.

And then there was the pettier level. Rand Paul might have wanted to talk about liberty, debt, and encroaching government, but instead he ended up in a war of words with a guy who wanted to talk about how he was a loser at the edge of the stage. Rand had a campaign built on libertarian ideas, but it didn't stand much of a chance against Trump's communication strategy of deliberate chaos.

Frame the conversation from your own perspective, and let others follow along. Frame problems from how you see them, and sometimes when the competition flares up, let your partners know those guys just aren't that important. When done honestly, it works.

And when done with a good, trusted team of people backing you up, you've got it made.

3

★

How to Keep Friends and Create Allies

Even before he won the presidency, Donald Trump had accomplished a good deal in his life. In many of the dramatic tellings, he, the leader, is front and center, making the deals, selling the brand, giving the speeches. But behind the scenes—and, increasingly, in the newspapers—the people around him and supporting him have played a critical role.

While Trump excels in one-on-one negotiations, few of his biggest successes or failures have taken place in a vacuum. The weeks, months, or years that have led to deals have benefited from the input of loyal hands and trusted advisers. And the same are on-site to see projects to their conclusions.

Nobody knows everything, and nobody can do everything—but successful people know how to surround themselves with a team that can make anything happen.

Trump did this to great effect in the business world and on the campaign trail, making sure to give his subordinates the leeway they needed and suffering no useless men or women.

"Behind the celebrity that was Donald was the business entity that was the Trump Organization," Timothy O'Brien writes in *Trump Nation*, "a teeny operation that catered to Donald's zealousness and preference for quick decisions."

"Small," "nimble," and "loyal" are three words that routinely describe Trump's teams, whether they were supporting the rising star of the 1970s, the famous businessman of the 1980s and '90s, the television star of the 2000s, or the presidential campaigner of the past few years.

"People thought we were this humongous firm with billions of people," Trump Organization executive Blanche Sprague recalled in *Trump Nation*. "In the New York office, there were only about eight or 10 close 'executives'; the rest were secretaries and accountants and everybody did everything. Your job was to make sure that everything got done."

"They help turn Trump's visions and deals into reality and perpetuate an image that admirers see as personifying the American Dream and critics see as a capitalist nightmare," the *Washington Post* reported in a September 1989 article titled "The Manager Behind The Mogul." "They protect him from the most far-fetched of ideas and prevent some plans from crashing in flames."

And whether talking to his longtime butler in Florida or

his doorman in New York City, the attribute Trump values highest is clear: loyalty.

RULE 11: The Difference Loyalty Makes

Corey Lewandowski was a political outsider. And not because he was some kind of intellectual rogue, bucking conservative orthodoxy, but because he'd helped a rogue New Hampshire senator who'd left the GOP two years prior run for Senate, once again on the Republican ticket. And as mentioned, that guy—an incumbent—lost in a day when that sort of thing was rare.

Corey had been a cop and dabbled in real estate while raising a sizable family. When he met Trump, he was on his way out the door at Charles Koch's Americans for Prosperity activist group. The future president was interested in his connections to right-wing activists (namely, the Kochs) and his understanding of politics in a state that was the second to vote in the Republican primaries.

In real life, Corey couldn't supply much with the Kochs—as he had actually burned bridges with anyone of import in that world—though he did know a thing or two about New Hampshire. In the end, he "gained Trump's trust by demonstrating he possessed the quality Trump values most," *New York* mag wrote: loyalty to Donald Trump.

When he'd signed on with Bob Smith, the doomed rogue senator, he'd shown this side. "Supporting Smith was sort of a blow-up-the-bridges-and-burn-the-boats decision, professionally," one top New Hampshire Republican told the *Washington Post*. And when Lewandowski had been warned about this by Smith himself, he replied, "I wear that as a badge of honor."

And he did, once even suggesting that the Lebanese heritage of John Sununu Jr., the favorite candidate of President George W. Bush, might mean he's sympathetic to terrorists.

This quality didn't seem to shine through during his time with Americans for Prosperity, unfortunately. Multiple Koch operatives told me he'd long been sidelined, and over beers a few strongly suggested he'd severely exaggerated his accomplishments to people both inside and outside the organization. Due to the Kochs' preference for keeping disagreements quietly in-house, however, few people knew this when the headlines blared that Trump had hired a captain of the powerful Koch network. And, once in Trump World, he was ever loyal to the boss.

Even after he was forced out in a power play by members of the Trump family, Lewandowski was still loyal, telling CNN's Dana Bash just hours later, "The campaign is moving in the right direction. That's the important thing.

"I know I've had a privilege and an honor of being part of this for the last eighteen or nineteen months and I have no regrets and I'm, I'm so thankful for this chance," he said. "And I know that what I will do moving forward is share my advice of what I know with Mr. Trump and his team if they want it. . . . And I can tell you that me and every person that I know will continue to vote for and support Donald Trump in any way possible."

"You're such a good soldier," Bash replied. "You're such a good soldier and your loyalty here is exactly why, one of the main reasons why Mr. Trump kept you on for so long."

Late on election night, the scene was surreal. While raucous supporters celebrated in the Midtown Hilton ballroom, Lewandowski was six blocks away, on a CNN panel belligerently demanding a mea culpa from everyone else, especially Van Jones—himself an early casualty of the Obama administration.

And he's still around, taking an office right near the White House, from where he and his partners peddle promises of access to a president he never crossed, even when fired.

Today, he may not have an office in the West Wing, but if you ask someone there if Corey is ever coming back, they'll laugh. "He's already here," they might say.

After they've been fired, close aides have an incredible ability to disrupt an operation they have intimate—and often embarrassing—knowledge of. Rarely has Trump been more endangered by that than when Roger Stone was pushed by the wayside.

Stone, who wears his Nixon tattoo proudly and describes himself as an "agent provocateur," was close to Trump for decades. "Roger saw something that nobody else saw back in the early '80s," Paul Manafort says in the Netflix documentary *Get Me Roger Stone*. "He created Donald Trump as a political figure," Jeffrey Toobin of the *New Yorker* chimed in.

"It's hard to assume he's not up to something, because he always is," Matt Labash wrote in a 2007 profile for the *Weekly Standard*. Even the D.C. people who don't take Stone very seriously—and there are quite a few of them—wouldn't want him as an enemy, and Trump was vulnerable.

But even he didn't attack the old boss, claiming he maintains a close relationship (Trump denies this) and traveling the country, promoting the cause each and every way he could, pushing Trump's case so provocatively that CNN and Fox News have uninvited him from TV at times.

"Those who say I have no soul, those who say I have no principles, are losers," he told Netflix's documentarians. "Those are bitter losers." Trump was a winner. And Stone had stood by him.

"In business, as a candidate and now as president, Mr. Trump has valued loyalty as the defining attribute in family, aides or Republicans in Congress," reports the *New York Times*.

And the loyal staff who've survived the turmoil and stayed closest even in the White House are the people Trump recruited from inside his own business operation.

"Loyal Aide in Trump Tower Acts as Gatekeeper," the *Times* declared in a long, flattering profile of Rhona Graff, the woman who has worked for him for thirty years.

"Mr. Trump can always count on Ms. Graff's allegiance," it reads, "and that has made Ms. Graff, from her office in Trump Tower, a major figure in the operations of the White House for a simple reason: She is believed to have a direct line to the president."

Keith Schiller, a longtime bodyguard, now serves as director of Oval Office operations, and was the trusted man chosen to deliver the news the FBI director was fired to James Comey himself (though Comey, it turned out, was out of town). His closeness to the now-president eventually led congressional investigators to list him as a witness when looking into allegations on Russian election interference.

Hope Hicks is another Trump Organization employee closely involved in the president's life. A young woman poached from another public relations job in only 2014, in January 2015, Trump called her to his office. "Mr. Trump looked at me and said, 'I'm thinking about running for president, and you're going to be my press secretary,'" she tells *New York* magazine.

A media gatekeeper on the trail, today she serves as the White House director of strategic communications and qualifies as the president's longest-serving political aide. Her mother wants her to put it all in a book.

Dan Scavino was a teenage caddie for Trump in 1990 when the businessman took a shine to him, eventually elevating him to a vice president and, now, to White House director of social media.

"We're all loyal to him," Scavino told CNN's Chris Moody. "And he's loyal to everybody that's with him. The retention of his employees at the Trump Organization is incredible—people don't leave Donald Trump."

Nine years before he met a teenage Scavino, Trump saw a security guard named Matthew Calamari taking care of hecklers at the U.S. Open. He liked how Calamari had handled the potentially chaotic situation decisively and professionally, and he hired him as a bodyguard.

Today, Calamari is the chief operating officer of the Trump Organization. His son, who followed in his dad's footsteps as a guard in 2011, is now in charge of surveillance for the whole company.

And the loyalty pays off for Donald Trump. Scavino scuttled his plan to open his own public relations firm so he could assist his boss on the campaign trail, and has served as an online voice for the man he first met nearly thirty years ago. "I know Mr. Trump's message very clearly, being around him eighteen hours a day, traveling around the country," he told CNN.

He's also fiercely protective: "Scavino talks about Trump like a devoted son defends the legacy of a father," Moody writes.

"It fires me up," Scavino says about attacks on his boss. "It pissed me off, it really does because I care about the man, I care about his family."

Today, Bill Procida is a vice president at the Trump Organization. He never went to college, but he wrote letters to

Trump asking for a chance. "If you're looking for someone to slam or slander Trump, you have the wrong guy," Procida said when *Politico* asked for an interview.

"He has said that every hire is a bit of a chance, that people with great credentials may not work out," Calamari told *Politico* magazine, "whereas those with lesser credentials often prove themselves to have great merit."

"Offering a lot of opportunity to people with not a lot of experience earned Trump loyalty in return," reporter Michael Kruse observed.

"Many of the people who are with me," Trump remarked to the *New York Times,* "have been with me for a long time."

Trump's team has been derided as politically inexperienced, and it's true. When *GQ* asked Trump if Hope's political inexperience might be a fresh and helpful attribute on the trail, he was blunt: "'No, I don't think there's a benefit to that,' he said flatly and frankly, 'but she was able to build political experience quickly. She was very natural.'"

And she had what he most valued—that loyalty.

There are very few true believers in politics, an openly transactional business where loyalty is rare and mercenary operatives are the norm. When deciding to join a campaign, people weigh the perceived chances of winning with the potential job it could mean for them if they pull it off. People often do this when joining a company in the private sector, too, of course, and as in politics, will bail when a business begins to fail.

The new job forced Trump to bring on a significantly larger team than he ever had before, and he absolutely suffered from this attitude among the career Republicans who joined him. The core team he can trust will prove essential to accomplishing anything in Washington.

Former Sen. Jim DeMint was one of the few true believers in conservative politics. He and Trump formed a good relationship on the trail after DeMint offered the esteemed Heritage Foundation's resources while a lot of others on the right were cold. After Trump won, he adopted the Heritage Foundation budget and pulled dozens of their people into his administration.

Then, when reports began to emerge that DeMint was being ousted by the board at Heritage over internal politics, Trump lauded DeMint for his help on confirming the president's first Supreme Court nominee, telling the audience at a National Rifle Association convention, "And also, from Heritage, Jim DeMint—it's been amazing. I mean, those people have been fantastic. They've been real friends."

Some wondered if Trump knew DeMint was in trouble at Heritage. He absolutely did, a man deeply involved in the communications told me. It was Trump's signal to the embattled DeMint team: Your friendship is not forgotten, and if you need it, there's a place for you in my White House.

Loyalty is something you can't teach, and it is easily among the most important attributes you can have in a friend, colleague, family member, or spouse. Without it, there's nothing. For me, trust is what separates a friend from an acquaintance, and when I hear people say, "They're my friend but yeah, I don't trust them," I shudder. How is it even possible to call someone a true friend without loyalty?

It's easy to find friends when you're winning, when you're on top. People emerge from all corners when you're the right person to know. The clearest way to tell who is real and who is not real is, of course, to fall and see who is there to help you up.

On March 26, 1991, when Trump was billions in debt and the self-described "poster boy for the recession," the *New York Times* and *Wall Street Journal* simultaneously ran front-page stories foretelling the end of Donald Trump.

"Anybody with a brain who read those stories would have said I was finished," Trump recalled in his book *The Art of the Comeback*. "The stories were picked up by radio and television and blasted throughout the world. This was by far the worst moment of my life.

"I was in my office, and there was dead silence. The phone had stopped ringing because even my closest friends felt it would be better to stay away from me rather than call in their regrets—something I always hated anyway. It was then that Rhona Graff, my very loyal secretary, came into my office and told me that Ivana was on the phone."

Already legally separated, Ivana wanted the money Trump owed her before he went belly-up. He'd done her wrong, and they eventually patched their relationship up (Ivana even remarried at Trump's Mar-a-Lago), but the line that stands out is when the phones stopped ringing and the newspapers said it was over: Donald Trump's "very loyal" secretary was still there, as she is today.

Hope Hicks "made a choice to work for the most fascist candidate in recent American history," a rival GOP candidate's tough-talking-yet-unsurprisingly-anonymous representative told *GQ* before Trump won the election. "Everyone who knows her tells her to stop doing this and putting her name on stuff. . . . She is going to regret everything she's said and done. And I don't think she knows it yet."

Hicks stood by her boss, and now they're both in the White House. Maybe it was smart of that GOP apparatchik to keep their name out of the papers.

But you don't need to lose billions or be called a fascist to get glimpses of who is really a loyal friend. It's the small things the boss might do that can give you a glimpse. Did they take credit for your work? Did they defend you in front of the top dogs when you were attacked? Did they buy you a beer when you had a rough day? If no, you can guess they won't stand beside you when your job is on the line.

And while it's good to be a receptive person, open to new people and willing to give second chances, it's dangerous to be too trusting. "I know this observation doesn't make any of us sound very good," Trump wrote in 2004, "but let's face the fact that it's possible that even your best friend wants to steal your spouse and your money."

And while second chances are an important part of a moral life, as the old adage goes, "Don't forget."

The key to others' loyalty to you—every single time—is your loyalty to others, of course. If you're there when your friends are down, if you show them you're standing with them even when they're hit, they'll do the same.

When CNN's Moody asked if there's anything that Trump could do to make the man he'd promoted from teen-age caddy to adult Trump Organization leader turn against him, Scavino thought for a moment and then replied, "No."

"I'm so loyal to the guy, I'm with him through thick and thin—no matter what happens."

But never take it for granted or let your friends' and co-workers' devotion get to your head—it is earned, never a right. And a lack of humility can get you in some trouble.

"I could stand in the middle of Fifth Avenue and shoot somebody and I wouldn't lose voters," Trump joked in an ill-advised moment at an Iowa campaign rally.

Now he's the president. And if there's one thing U.S. presidents know about shooting people, it's some things are better to delegate.

RULE 12: Delegate, Don't Micromanage

The best part of having a team that you built is using it. People you trust and who are loyal to you, people who know you and can anticipate what you would like to see done, people committed to the company or the project. They're hard to come by, but once you get a team moving cohesively and in a way you can rely on, there's little better.

The ability to plan long-term is completely reliant on the luxury of taking your eyes off the road. If you can move your focus from what is immediately in front you and look at the maps, scan the horizon, and think "Where do I need to get?" you're golden. But if every time you take your hand off the wheel, your team lets you down, you're in trouble.

In contrast to having a good team, when you have people you can't rely on and you ask them to work on a project, when you come back you just might find the amount of work and time you have to put into unscrewing the situation would have taken care of the project in the first place. It's a rough place to be, and while TV might say otherwise, firing people stinks. It simply isn't fun, and the extra effort put into hiring and recruiting people you won't have to get rid of is absolutely worthwhile.

Even the man who made "You're fired" an American catchphrase doesn't really like to do it, often handing the difficult task to deputies. "He didn't like firing people," Barbara Res, who was the project manager for building Trump Tower, told *Politico* magazine.

More important, as Trump learned quick and hard, the failure of any member of the team is a failure for you.

Representatives Diane Black and Markwayne Mullin promised they'd have Obamacare repeal on Trump's desk by

February 20, and Trump, the leader of their party and the country, backed their optimism. Months later, after one public failure and a lot of public bickering, repeal still languished in the Senate.

It's likely the businessman, who has complained about dealing with the Japanese because of how many executives they bring to a negotiation, underestimated the moving parts that have to work in cohesion to push a bill to his desk. It's certain he underestimated the difficulty of the effort, even if a month later he called it "such an easy one." And it's equally certain he took the brunt of the blame.

Was it hard-line conservatives who cost him the bill or liberal Republicans? Democratic opposition or bad advice in his own war room? Was it his own hubris? In all likelihood, it was all of these things, but in reality, any one of them could have sunk the bill, and a failed deal for the boss's company is a failure for the boss.

All these moving parts, and his public disdain for them, might be a reason Donald Trump isn't really big on delegating tasks. He doesn't like to let big things out of his own sites, and it doesn't come naturally to him.

In past presidential campaigns, guys like Mitt Romney—someone perfectly capable of being tough over a long career in business in politics—chose to delegate the role of attack dog to surrogates. Men like Govs. John Sununu (father of the Sununu Lewandowski attacked) and Chris Christie hit the trail and cable shows to lob bombs, swinging hard and generally being vicious to the opposition. It's common practice in politics to delegate the attack-dog roles. Clinton, Obama, Bush—they all deployed pundits and politicians to the front lines to play the bad cop while they themselves focused on the broader, happier message of uniting the country, moving ahead, or some other witless trope.

Trump did not. While men like Rudy Giuliani happily volunteered for the job of campaign mad dog, Trump declined to rely on them, seeing himself as his best attacker and launching barbs, insults, and threats on a near-daily basis.

Not only was Donald better at it, but unlike with surrogates, many of whom are retired politicians or pundits without much name recognition, when Trump lobbed an attack it could dominate the news cycle. He's a smart guy, but no one was interrupting Ted Cruz on the campaign trail to respond to something CNN's Jeffrey Lord said. It was Trump's utterances that made the news.

On social media, it was much of the same. In the past, politicians like President Obama have signed their own tweets to show they were different from the ones their staff had sent out, but with Trump, nearly everything came directly from him. He trusts Dan Scavino and Justin McConney, who runs the Trump Organization's social media, to take care of the accounts and help grow their follows, just like he trusted Giuliani to hit hard on his behalf, but in the same vein, Trump knows he's the best at it there is. In this, as in a lot of places, he has a support staff, but he never really takes his eyes off the road.

The most visible example might be his former spokesman, Sean Spicer. Spicer had what looked like an enviable job: He had risen from C-level political notoriety to command the live afternoon airtime of every cable news station in the country, with his every tweet and utterance echoed for days in millions of living rooms across the country. He's basically a TV star, and just a year ago he was the abused head of communications for the Republican Party's support group.

But the job isn't cushy by a long stretch, and while a lot of folks in D.C. might switch places with him, they know they wouldn't love their lives any more if they did, because the boss is watching like a hawk, and as with the above, there's little his surrogates can do to outperform him in communicating.

Early in Spicer's tenure, Trump privately griped about everything from his energy levels to his suit and tie choice, critical of it all. When Spicer overadjusted to fit what President Trump wanted, *Saturday Night Live* saw a chance to be funny for the first time since the early 1990s and made him into a character. Then Trump didn't like that the character was played by a woman. With NBC and MSNBC parroting their own company's skits making fun of Spicer like they're news, any one of us can see it's not a good place for him to be, and Spicer wasn't there for long.

When put in a place where you're asked to do something the boss would rather be doing, and indeed the boss loves doing, it's your time to shine. And if you don't, you can be sure the boss will know about it. It's a difficult place to be, but one that, if you succeed, you can capitalize on. Spicer's trouble was that Trump preferred sparring with the press to being holed up in his office, so he never wanted to delegate the task. In other places, he'd prefer a trusted executive.

"Trump keeps a close eye on the executives, echoing a hands-on management style that his father displayed as a builder, owner, and manager of thousands of rent-controlled apartments in Brooklyn and Queens," the *Washington Post* reported in a 1989 article. "Executives say Trump gives them plenty of room to maneuver, but he personally signs hundreds of checks a week, reviews about 100 documents, often phones the same people that his managers will be calling that day and repeatedly quizzes the managers about details of projects."

Donald Trump has long struggled with delegating tasks he enjoys or does very well himself. Where he's stood out is in empowering his executives to move freely on their own volition, crafting deals and creating situations he can capitalize on.

James Capalino served as a commissioner and adviser to Trump's old-time New York City rival, Mayor Ed Koch. But by the time the *Post* was profiling The Donald, Capalino had left government and was advising the business magnate. "In the spirit of a benevolent despot," Capalino observed, "he has created a very exciting, very challenging work climate that gives senior executives a great deal of latitude, a great deal of responsibility, but in a framework where no one is operating under any misapprehensions about where the buck starts and where the buck stops."

The president isn't famous for big teams of executives, but he is famous for relying on the team he has when he can. And when he can't, he'll rely on himself. When British Prime Minister Theresa May visited the United States, for example, among other things she was eager to discuss was international trade. Her country had just sent trade with their biggest commercial partner into flux by voting to leave the European Union; could she rely on their old friends in the United States? Especially after the new president had promised to critically review the existing agreements?

The job would normally fall to the U.S. trade secretary, a trusted position on the president's handpicked, Senate-confirmed cabinet. The snag was that Wilbur Ross, a billionaire banker who would become Trump's secretary of commerce, hadn't been confirmed yet.

And when there's no one else you can trust to do it, it falls on the boss to do it himself.

"I don't have my commerce secretary," Trump griped, concluding, "They want to talk trade, so I'll have to handle it myself."

Trump has the international business background to discuss the matter with May, and was a fine pinch hitter. But sometimes in his career he's come across things he knows nothing about—and some of his great successes have come from relying on the guys who know a thing or two.

So when he got the Wollman Rink project, he found the guys who knew how to do it. He had no choice but to bring someone on, but whereas the city had, for example, hired refrigeration experts instead of rink experts to consult on what was going wrong, Trump hired the best professional rink builders in Canada. And where the city was no closer to completing the project after six years, Trump completed the project in six months.

Donald Trump might have learned this lesson years before the Wollman Rink episode, when building Trump Tower. Today, he happily points to its construction as one of his great accomplishments, but at the time, he'd never built a skyscraper from start to finish. And since engineering a 664-foot tower is not an easy thing to learn on the fly, he had to rely on people who already knew how.

"He had no choice but to trust us," architect John Barie recalled to *Politico* thirty-three years later. "Being new to the design and construction process, he was very much involved. He was hands-on in the sense of knowing what was going on. In terms of decision-making, he delegated a great deal to [construction manager] Barbara Res," who acted on his behalf.

"He said I would be like a 'Donna Trump,'" Res wrote in a memoir, *All Alone on the 68th Floor: How One Woman*

Changed the Face of Construction, "and I would treat everything as if it were my project."

Res "was the first woman put in charge of a skyscraper in New York," Trump recalls. "She was half the size of most of these bruising guys, but she wasn't afraid to tell them off when she had to, and she knew how to get things done."

Though as both Res and Barie mentioned, even with good people in place, Trump would check in frequently. "You have to be very rough and very tough with most contractors or they'll take the shirt right off your back," Trump writes on a call he made to someone working on Trump Parc, luxury condominiums just off Central Park.

Trump told the man in charge of demolition on Trump Parc that he needed him personally involved, and that if he didn't get this done in a way that satisfied Trump, he'd never work for him again. Then he got the number-two guy in charge of concrete on the phone, telling him all the problems he'd heard of with uneven floors and letting him know how much future business was in it for them if they got the job done right.

The ideal situation, of course, is building a team of executives who can act on your behalf without phone calls and threats. People who will do the job because they're good, loyal people.

The day after he was elected, Trump promised to "call upon the best and brightest to leverage their tremendous talent for the benefit of all." But for a candidate who had about

10 percent of the staff Hillary Clinton's did, coming from a business famous for its lean executive offices and into a massive government, it's a tall task. And it's a task made even more difficult by the number of seasoned Republicans who had been viciously critical of Trump during the campaign.

"Friends say assembling high-performing teams is one of the president-elect's strengths," NPR reported days after the election surprise, quoting Colony Capital CEO Tom Barrack as well as Ivanka Trump in support.

"He pushes everybody around him, including you, through comfort barriers that they never thought they could ever shatter," Barrack said during his convention speech the summer before.

"Competence in the building trades," Ivanka said at the same convention, "is easy to spot. And incompetence is impossible to hide."

Trump grabbed headlines for saying he just might know more than the generals, but when it came down to action, the former high school military cadet knew about as much about war as he'd known about ice rinks. He knew this key thing: We've been losing when we should be winning. And he knew that there were winners out there.

So one of his first major staffing choices, and one that was lauded by leaders in both parties in Washington, was storied Marine Corps General James "Mad Dog" Mattis.

Mattis is legendary for his tough-yet-intellectual leadership, and known as "the warrior monk." Retired Lieutenant Colonel Ralph Peters wrote in the *New York Post* that "Mattis may be the finest four-star on duty in any service today."

"He's certainly the humblest," Peters continued. "And maybe the smartest—but he'll let you figure that out for yourself."

A good person in the right place won't only do a great job, they can be relied on for advice, and a media fretting if Trump would take advice from anyone was, at least for a second, assuaged. Putting good people in the right spot isn't just good for them, it's essential to your success.

Mattis got to work quickly reorganizing how America's wards will be fought, giving increased ability to act and react to military field commanders. Those field commanders then turned around and absolutely lit up the foe, dropping ordnance so large on ISIS's heads that North Korea, Iran, and the rest of the perennial problem states sat up and took notice.

When Trump promised to "bomb the sh-t out of" ISIS, the self-serious punditry scoffed, saying that was an unreasonable thing to say. It's more complicated, they howled, than that.

The men Trump put in charge of America's wars didn't seem to think so.

A second thing essential to success is not letting yourself get bogged down in the details. Managing the American military is an incredibly intense job, rivaled only by our Department of State and beaten only by the Oval Office. As past presidents have been quick to point out, by the very nature of the office, only the toughest decisions in the entire government come to the president of the United States.

Jimmy Carter denies it, but the folks in the White House knew it was true: He spent time looking so closely over the shoulders of his people that he personally approved or disallowed use of the White House tennis courts. It's no good for you, it's no good for morale, and it's no good for your mission.

And if one of your trusted people can't hack it, well, they'll just need to go.

RULE 13: Fire People Early and Often

It strikes people as funny that Donald Trump doesn't actually like to fire people, considering he made "You're fired" a tagline for his show.

Billy Procida, who was a vice president in Trump's company in the 1990s, told *Politico* magazine he'd never even heard the phrase.

"I have never heard him say the words 'You're fired' to anyone," Procida said. "He really doesn't fire people. He makes it known he doesn't want you there, and you move on."

The article tells the story of the top chef at Mar-a-Lago.

He made a fancy Caesar salad in a parmesan bowl that surely took a long time. By the chef's story, Trump wasn't in a good mood when he came into the kitchen and told the staff he expected a salad to be lettuce, tomatoes, and the rest in a regular bowl.

The chef likely knew that the traditional Caesar salad doesn't have tomatoes, but instead of bearing the boss's annoyance and explaining this later, he chose to embarrass Donald Trump and say, "I didn't know you were the new executive chef."

Trump didn't address the insubordination right then and there, but upon leaving the kitchen he informed the chef's manager he didn't want to see that man on his staff again. The tale might come across as harsh, but it contains important realities for both how to handle the person you're working for and how to handle the people working for you.

On its face, insubordination to a superior cannot stand in any circumstance. Sometimes, of course, insubordination takes on a different level in different environments. In our newsroom, for example, it's not uncommon for curses to fly, beers to get cracked, and pushback to be given to a boss's idea. In some offices, that won't do at all. In all offices—ours included—the kind shown by the chef, the kind that shows a real disrespect, will not fly ever. Only way it ever really could fly is if it was your ass flying to the curb, but the federal government won't let that move go these days. Maybe someday.

When you've got a point to make to your boss (and the chef did), keep your peace until you can share it. We can never be sure, but if the chef's manager had whispered to Trump at a later time that the reason the salad was served this way was tradition, and a house salad would surely accommodate tomatoes, things might have turned out differently.

Trump doesn't like to fire people because very, very few people really do. It's in everyone's interest to keep the boat steady. If you've ever worked at a restaurant, you know the chaos that can be caused by missing a single person on a busy night—forget about the executive chef. You might as well light your hair on fire and break your feet, because that's how you'll feel by the end of the shift.

The reason anyone in a position of real authority will eventually have to make the tough call to let another person go is because the wrong person in place can poison the company and everything the rest of your team is working toward.

Roger Stone is an interesting case. Before anyone else, Stone saw in Trump a political figure. Or at least that's the narrative. Maybe, as Stone puts it, he simply was "a jockey looking for a horse."

For years he'd served a close, if not entirely clear, role for Donald Trump, promoting his boss (and himself) while attacking his boss's (and his own) enemies. Whether Trump was up, down, or in between, Stone hit hard, spreading rumors, undermining competition, and generally and happily sowing chaos.

"He loves the game, he has fun with it, and he's very good at it," Trump told Netflix.

"America may be collapsing," Tucker Carlson told the same documentarians, "but Roger Stone is determined to enjoy it."

Stone was the right man for that moment, and he drummed up a lot of support. He was also a tempestuous man, and Trump believed he sought too much publicity for himself. He'd been fired from campaigns in the past for threatening a man's dad, he wanted everyone in the world to know Bill Clinton was a rapist and his wife enabled him, and he admitted he'd had too many martinis when, after he was off the campaign, he called Roland Martin "a fat negro."

He did not, however, apologize to Ana Navarro, stating, quite correctly, "I don't understand why she's there, given her lack of qualifications."

And as the campaign progressed, the choice for Trump was to keep going Stone's way, or gear up for a national contest with Hillary Clinton.

Donald Trump says he doesn't talk to Stone anymore, though it's hard to know if that's true. Whether he quit or was fired, the attack dog that had to be let go remained loyal. Another reason to do your firings in quiet on the side is that it's a little less public. No reason to air any more dirty laundry than you must.

It's worth never forgetting, too, that fealty and loyalty are not the same thing.

Fealty is external; it is something you swear—a solemn promise you make. In feudal times, a knight might take an oath of fealty to his lord in which he would commit himself to faithful service.

Loyalty is internal; it is something you have—it comes from within. The dictionary defines it as "a strong feeling of support or allegiance." In other words, it's a feeling of something—not an obligation to something.

In the world of business and politics, there are a lot of people with neither, and they're easy to spot. It's the people who swear fealty who might be more difficult to pinpoint.

It's easy to assume a character as unpredictable as Stone simply swore fealty, but his actions since tell another story. Other cases are a little more clear-cut.

If you were watching the news that day or the next, you remember Governor Chris Christie pledging fealty.

"I am proud to be here to endorse Donald Trump for president of the United States," Christie said shortly after dropping out, at a late February rally at Trump's Mar-a-Lago club.

"I will lend my support between now and November in every way that I can for Donald to help to make this campaign an even better campaign than it's already been," he added, just weeks after the world had watched him impersonating Trump and calling him a fantasist who is unfit to lead.

It's true, that can be the nature of politics and even business, though it's often less public. But it was unseemly enough that the Internet jokesters had a blast with it. Over the next few days, as stories flew of snubs and poor tempers, it didn't look like there was any real bond of loyalty growing between the two men. Still, Christie had taken his licks to support the boss and was also the most experienced Republican executive on the team, so when it came time to tap a leader for Donald Trump's effort to staff his potential administration, Christie was an obvious choice.

Once he was elected, the campaign switched its focus and the calculus changed. Christie, Trump's camp suggested, had been staffing the transition to his own tune, bringing in friends and his own loyalists all while his own scandals at home piled up (Christie, for his part, disputes this). Questions on loyalty, baggage, and decision making piled up, and with Trump second-guessing the governor's motives, he was unceremoniously replaced with a more trusted hand, Vice President–elect Mike Pence.

Folks who have worked anywhere, really, will come across a phenomenon that is pronounced and insufferable in any situation, but especially politics: that thing that makes people think they're indispensable.

There's little doubt the fancy chef with the parmesan bowls thought that he was indispensable. That, or he hated his job so much he wanted to get fired. He mouthed off and he was shown the door, and while Mar-a-Lago's fine fare is above a reporter's pay grade, I haven't heard any grumbling about the club's offerings being anything but delicious. He was not, it appears, so indispensable.

Christie, in that vein, appeared even more important than an executive chef is to a restaurant, but when Trump came around, he didn't like what he saw and he moved quickly and decisively, axing people he thought were ignoring his campaign directive to "drain the swamp."

"The graveyards of the world are filled with indispensable men," French leader Charles de Gaulle observed after World War II.

But to expand on his point, the graveyards of the world are full, period. One thing that will keep your career out of them longer is a right hand you can count on.

RULE 14: Have a Good Right-Hand Man

Donald Trump is a lot of things to a lot of people, but there's not a person out there who can say he is not an independent man.

Trump is less connected than any other president in modern history to political party, and he doesn't owe his career to any politician. Indeed, he's spent nearly his entire life either butting heads with politicians or giving them reasons to owe him.

But in the race for the U.S. presidency, that had to change. In a political game, a little politics are in order. And when you're planning to take your hand off the ship's wheel to drop bombs all over the game, it's important to have a good tillerman.

When Donald Trump was first in the market for a right hand, he was still regarded with a healthy suspicion by conservatives, the Christian right, and professional Republicans in general. And while he mulled over who he would rely on to represent him on the campaign trail and on Capitol Hill as his vice president, it became clearer he needed someone who would soothe those party concerns—someone who had assets that Trump lacked.

In the end, his choices came down to two men: New Jersey Gov. Chris Christie or Indiana Gov. Mike Pence.

It was a tough choice. Donald Trump had known Christie for fourteen years, but his friend was a northeast politician who had inspired the ire of all different stripes of conservatives, was snagged in a traffic scandal of his own doing, and had alienated a good many people with his penchant for theatrically hogging the camera.

A right-hand man should be a hedge, holding attributes the leader lacks. Christie, to his detriment, didn't have anything Trump lacked, carried political baggage Trump had avoided, and could be unpredictable—anything but the steady hand the freewheeling nominee for president needed.

"Advisers and family members stressed over and over to Mr. Trump that he was selecting a running mate to unite the Republican Party, not a new best friend," the *New York Times* reported just after his decision was announced.

And so that's what Trump did, announcing Mike Pence, a twelve-year congressman and first-term governor from Indiana whom Trump had very little history with, and who is essentially the opposite of him in every sense. And the news did exactly what he needed.

"Trump wasn't hunting for a kindred spirit," *Time* magazine observed. "By tapping Pence for the role, he's getting a movement conservative out of central casting, a seasoned politician whose selection may soothe Republicans still skeptical that Trump is one of them."

"Conservative leaders greeted the decision with enthusiasm," the D.C. newspaper *Roll Call* reported, "saying the Indiana governor, who served six terms in the House, has been a consistent champion of economic and social conservative causes."

"In Mr. Pence, the presumptive Republican nominee has found a running mate with unimpeachable conservative credentials, warm relationships in Washington and a vast reservoir of goodwill with the Christian right," the *Times* chipped in.

"He can help Trump navigate the halls of Congress," *Time* magazine agreed.

And the move brought some much-needed praise from the heads of the Republican Senate and House.

Donald Trump had long given a clear vision of both his own ambitions and the country's problems, but he'd struggled with how to get there. Pence was the perfect man for the job. He'd been a radio host, a congressman, and then a state's top executive. He stuck to his principles even when they were unpopular.

The first time I met Mike Pence, he was defending his strong stance against legalized marijuana to a small gathering of leading D.C. libertarians—in other words, not simply a crew in disagreement with the then congressman, but a very smart crew in disagreement, all of whom figured they were important enough to argue. Pence didn't dodge them— he confronted them without even seeming confrontational. It was an impressive introduction.

And everything we've learned about the midwesterner who looks like *Johnny Quest*'s Race Bannon supports this impression. When you need a man you can rely on, he's your guy.

And for Donald Trump—a man who doesn't care to share too much of his spotlight—Pence's understated humility would keep him out of trouble. Indeed, in the months since the administration began, he's one of the only characters who haven't gotten into any trouble.

In his debut performance, Pence handily sidestepped Hillary's VP choice, Tim Kaine, deftly defending the ticket every step of the way. To turn on the news the next day, you'd think he'd tossed a stick into the Democrats' fixed-gear bicycle wheel, sending them flying, skinny arms flailing, into the warm concrete.

Even Trump's sworn enemies in the media—you may have noticed there are a good deal of those—admitted his performance was "unflappable," as he "calmly sidestepped" pointed attacks.

Pence had his share of frustrations. One reporter who spent an afternoon with him told me the mood was frustrated at best as the unfailingly polite governor waited hours for his late boss to wrap up in New York.

Not long after, Mike Pence heard that his new boss has talked about grabbing women "by the p - - sy." Keep in mind, Mike Pence is a devout man whom feminists and their weak-wristed male "allies" criticized for feeling improper when dining alone with female employees. Keep in mind there was controversy over whether he said "sh-t" during a campaign stop, and the consensus was a likely "no."

Still, when the beta anti-Trump Republicans called on Pence to ditch Trump, and the slightly-less-beta anti-Trump Republicans called on him to lead a revolt against his boss, he said no. He was clearly angry, and he publicly admitted he was disappointed, but he resisted all calls to leave the man he'd promised to run with.

Mike Pence, always loyal, stood at his post, steadfastly guiding the ship into the storm even when everyone else was predicting disaster, and despite the flailing of the professional Republican class. He has come out the stronger for it.

As the long campaign wound down, *National Review*—a conservative magazine that openly loathed The Donald—profiled Pence on the trail, opening the scene with the VP's plane skidding off a rainy runway at New York's LaGuardia Airport.

"It's telling that while many of his allies are bearish about what Election Day will bring, Pence is certain that a historic triumph is at hand," *National Review* reported.

"I really believe—I really believe—that we're on our way to a victory," Pence told the writer.

"Of course, it's impossible to survey the wreckage from inside the plane," the author remarked five days before the ticket's historic win. No doubt he was very impressed with his wit on that one. Writers often are.

"At midnight, it was too early to tell how big his decision paid off," his hometown paper, the *Indianapolis Star,* reported at 11:59 p.m.—the last minute of Election Day. "Trump was overperforming in states like Wisconsin he hadn't been projected to carry and the race was too close to call."

"Win or lose, Pence has mostly maintained that optimism throughout, despite a lot of campaign turbulence."

Thirty minutes later, I stood on the sidewalk outside Clinton's campaign party thinking about a cold beer while Daily Caller News Foundation reporter Blake Neff quizzed Clinton's supporters, who were scattered about as they stumbled and crumbled out of the Javits Center, tears in their eyes.

Ten weeks later, I stood on the stairs of the Capitol as Donald Trump and his right-hand man were sworn into office. In front of me, a friend, top aide to a Republican senator and all-around never-Trumper, admitted, "My mother called and told me I'd better get my butt down here and see history."

Trump had led the charge, no doubt, but the two men had gotten to that place together, and in the months after, Pence's own strengths shone through. At one of the pivotal early moments of Trump's presidency, Paul Ryan was unable to get Obamacare repeal through his own chamber. At this moment, Trump turned to Mike Pence, who had the reputation and the experience to negotiate its passage. He got it done, and Trump then blasted it at the Senate.

And even while Trump faced leaks from dueling White House factions and attacks from within his administration, it's impossible to miss that no one has fingered Pence—his office has stayed above it.

And Trump has remained loyal to his vice president in return. While he'd stood by his embattled national security advisor, Mike Flynn, longer than many of his allies would have liked, he swiftly fired the general when he discovered Flynn had lied to Pence.

Donald Trump and Mike Pence are openly different, but they play off each other. In Pence, Trump had a steady colleague, trusted and reliable. Someone who stood by him without reinforcing mistakes he made along the way. Someone who had capital where Trump lacked it, and who could reach out to Republicans, conservatives, and political Christians, pulling those hard-to-pin-down groups around the campaign when it was needed. A guy who would help with hiring and firing, lead teams without being worried about, and never embarrass the boss.

It might be hard to identify someone like that in your own life. If you find them, hold on to them—your loyalty will be rewarded ten times. But for most of us, the people we have to rely on are our family.

RULE 15: Trust in Family

It's both obvious and cliché to say that Donald Trump's earliest influences were his family, so I shouldn't.

But Donald Trump's earliest influences were his family. His father, in particular, weighed heavily on the young man, and has throughout his life, from his work ethic to his mannerisms and focused drive.

Fred Trump never went to college—he didn't have the luxury. His father—Donald Trump's grandfather—was a hard worker but also a hard liver, and he passed when the kids were young. Shortly after high school, Fred started a company in his mother's name, Elizabeth Trump & Son, or E. Trump & Son, because he himself was too young to sign checks.

He would build a small house, sell it, and put the profits toward building more houses, expanding all the while. He turned this into a lucrative life, sending his younger brother to study science in college, becoming a real estate lord of New York's working-class burrows, and building a strong business to raise his children in.

He could also be demanding, according to the family's oral histories.

"On Sunday mornings, he would drop all of his children off at the house of his sister, Elizabeth, and ask his brother-in-law, who worked six days a week, to check his books," the *New York Times* reports. "To avoid Fred, the family started attending an earlier church service, said John Walter, his sister's son, who eventually did his uncle's books."

In addition to his work-all-the-time approach to life, he was a sharp dresser and, while not as flashy as his son, did once literally rent a showboat to cruise Coney Island's beaches blasting patriotic music and sending coupons for homes he'd built floating toward the shore. He called them "Trump Homes," naming larger developments by the Trump name as well.

The whole time, Donald was watching. "I learned about toughness in a very tough business," Donald writes in his first book. "I learned about motivating people, and I learned about competence and efficiency: Get in, get it done, get it done right, and get out."

Donald also performed well under the pressure, acknowledging that it might have been his own contentment with a businesslike relationship with his dad that allowed the two to get along so well. Donald's brother, Freddy, was eight years Donald's senior and not made for the pressures Fred and Donald thrived in. Freddy's eventually fatal battle with alcohol weighed heavily on his younger brother, and was likely influential in Donald's order that his children not partake themselves.

Donald and Freddy's father was old-school. He played the political games he felt he had to, but had no time for Manhattan or the fancy materials that built it. When he came out to look at Trump Tower on Fifth Avenue, Donald recalls, he asked, "Why don't you forget about the damn glass? Give them four or five stories of it and then use common brick for the rest."

"Nobody," Fred asserted confidently, "is going to look up anyway."

Donald Trump was looking upward—and outward—but he took the lessons he'd learned with him and instilled them in his own family. And a very successful family it is.

Critics often point to Donald Trump's three marriages as proof he isn't any ideal of a family man. The *New York Times* article on his father even quotes Donald recalling his father's humorous ribbing, "one place you'll never beat me is with the marriage stuff."

"President Donald Trump," CNN jokes, "has a modern American family tree: a wife, five children from three marriages, two daughters-in-law and a son-in-law, eight grandchildren, and two ex-wives."

There were rough spots for sure, and much of the country tuned in while lawsuits and gossip dominated his relationships, but today, Donald Trump's relationship with Ivana and Marla Maples appears amicable. Both Donald Trump's ex-wives were in happy attendance at his inauguration. Ivana Trump, Donald's first wife, kept the Trump name (despite being married once prior) and even remarried at his Mar-a-Lago club. And along nearly the entire campaign trail, his children were close behind him, with the older three sharing the spotlight and following their father into power. Their reliable character, then and now, is an exception to an issue common with raising children with as much money as they were raised with.

There's a hard-to-miss problem at the top: A lot of the superrich have superawful kids. As a bloodthirsty public that doesn't care much for royalty, our tabloids have a sort of fascination with these tragic tales.

"The truth is," Nathaniel Hawthorne wrote in his classic book *The House of the Seven Gables*, "that once in every half-century, at least, a family should be merged into the great, obscure mass of humanity, and forget about its ancestors."

Leonardo DiCaprio's character in *The Departed* summarized this antiaristocratic sentiment well, noting, "Families are always rising and falling in America, am I right?"

And yet the older Trump children of a billionaire father divorced from their mother and obsessed with his work are remarkably well adjusted.

A trick Donald Trump cites is leading by example. One of America's many unsuccessful antidrug public education campaigns urged parents to be a "#1 Hypocrite" and crack down on the foolish decisions their pain-in-the-butt kids make—even if they'd made those same decisions when they were younger pains in their own parents' butts. Trump skips that step, leading the life himself.

"The world is so tough and it is so competitive that you can't put yourself, as a child, or even as a parent, if you want that child to be successful, at a disadvantage of letting them drink or letting them take drugs because it is not going to work," Trump told a crowd at a New Hampshire town hall.

"If you don't drink and you don't do drugs, your children . . . are going to have a tremendously enhanced chance of really being successful and having a good life," said the man who became the first president since H. W. Bush to abstain from drug use.

Their drive, compounded by their reliability, has allowed Donald Trump to rely on his children more than any other president in modern history. Eric Trump and Donald Trump Jr. were both old enough—and ready enough—to take the reins of their father's company when he left the driver's seat for politics. And his ability to trust them to lead without his constant guidance is a rare thing in an age of graduates living in Mom's basement.

Indeed, their guidance was key during the campaign, where he relied on them to work through major decisions and, sometimes, scandals.

When the people Trump had relied on, like Lewandowski and Manafort, let him down, it was his family who were there to identify the problems and work through them.

Lewandowski was the first. Summoned to a Trump Tower meeting with the family, *New York* magazine reports he was interrogated by the Trump children, including Ivanka, over the campaign's lack of infrastructure and other failings.

"Their father grew visibly upset as he heard the list of failures," *New York* reported. "Finally, he turned to Lewandowski and said, 'What's your plan here?'"

Basically incapable of running a campaign outside of media coverage, Lewandowski reportedly suggested leaking the VP pick as a cure for the bad press—and his own weak performance. "And with that, Lewandowski was out."

"It was ultimately Ivanka Trump who sat down with her father on Sunday and convinced him to let Lewandowski go," CNN heaped on, "even offering an ultimatum of sorts about her own continued involvement with the campaign, according to sources with knowledge of this conversation."

Lewandowski's successor, political veteran Paul Manafort, was a different case. Manafort's own set of children worried a great deal about their father's past dealings with corrupt foreign rulers—and how his high profile on the campaign might expose that and hurt him. Those worries were leaked by criminal hackers who exposed private conversations between his daughters, so it's difficult to know if they ever advised their dad as to their worries, but his eventual resignation from the campaign and the months of scandal that followed show they were maybe wiser than Dad was in the moment.

"He is the best at what he does," Jessica Manafort texted in a conversation reported in *Politico*, but the relationship could be poison for the family, they concluded. Even when we can be too consumed with our work and ambitions, the family that knows us best can be an essential check.

After Manafort tendered his resignation, Eric Trump was the campaign's most visible spokesman, telling Fox News, "My father just didn't want to have the distraction looming over the campaign and quite frankly looming over all the issues that Hillary's facing right now."

Months later in the White House, a dangerous campaign has become a dangerous world, and more than ever, the president relies on his family, with daughter Ivanka even keeping an office in the West Wing and her husband, Jared Kushner, taking on the role of political officer and confidant, both enforcing loyalty to the president and advising his father-in-law.

The role family plays in Trump's White House has irked partisan Democrats who are quick to forget another president who, as I wrote at the end of 2016, followed a very similar path toward creating a political dynasty.

"Donald Trump," I wrote at the *Daily Caller,* "is not the first president to get a head start from dad, be worth a billion dollars, or even bring members of his nuclear family into the White House as close advisers. Indeed, another president did all of those things—and not a Founding Father or some forgotten 19th-century bureaucrat, but a television man."

That man was John F. Kennedy, who came from a wealthy and driven father and appointed his brother Robert attorney general of the United States despite a noticeable lack of legal experience.

The press nicknamed Kennedy's White House family "Camelot"—a name still invoked today.

"I just wanted to give him a little legal practice before he becomes a lawyer," JFK joked about his brother, who was thirty-five—a year younger than Trump's son-in-law when Kushner accepted a job in the White House.

What connected Jared Kushner and Bobby Kennedy in the eyes of their bosses was not just the valuable advice they'd provided on the campaign trail, but their unquestionable loyalty to their family.

"There is nothing to compare with family if they happen to be competent, because you can trust family in a way you can never trust anyone else," Trump wrote in *The Art of the Deal.*

Every person we come across every day, from the boss to

the coworker, and from the politician in D.C. to the street beggar just outside, has their own game to play. Those of us lucky enough to have a family have another thing that binds us—we're all taking care of our own.

In his famous tome *Leviathan,* English philosopher Thomas Hobbes noted that outside of society, "the life of man" is "solitary, poor, nasty, brutish, and short." Society itself is built on family, and without family in our lives, it can indeed sometimes be a sort of "every man for himself."

Nothing guards us more from that sort of dystopia than the family. Friends—even great friends—come and go. They can be trusted, but rarely as well as even a close family member who otherwise annoys the heck out of you. All of us, if we've lived long enough, have close friends and even family who have let us down. And in that same vein, a lot of us have family who have let us down when it really counted. But throughout the years, it's still that family—and not those long-lost friends—who provide the foundation for our success. And, importantly, they will protect your from yourself, your enemies, and the morons you've taken a shine to.

Once you've got your house in order, it's time to look outward. Communication is the first move.

4

☆

Get Your Message Out

Donald Trump never had any trouble communicating what was on his mind.

In 1980, he gave an early television interview to *The Today Show,* in which a young Tom Brokaw told viewers about the $11 million apartments available in the incoming Trump Tower and wondered if Trump would buy the World Trade Center next.

"I had a great faith in New York," Trump replied.

Then thirty-three, Donald Trump was new to television, but was already crafting the message he wanted to be broadcast to viewers nationwide. Reserved, even seeming a little shy at times, the young developer considered each response carefully before putting forth what he wanted to communicate.

Six presidents and nearly forty years later, Trump looms larger than ever. One hundred million Americans have been born, empires have crumbled, and whole world orders have passed while Donald Trump has beamed into American living rooms, and today any attempt to block his words and actions out of your life would require a hunter-gatherer lifestyle in the Black Hills.

In those decades, Trump has formed a unique bond with the American people. While living a life we can charitably call glitzy and flashy, he has spoken plainly in a familiar style nearly all of us recognize, and we've listened.

Despite a life on the screen, little has been scripted. Those few things that have—cameos in movies like *Home Alone 2: Lost in New York*—are the rare moments that have come off as stiff. The rest—"reality" game shows, newspaper feuds, arena rallies, and Sean Hannity interviews—are authentic Trump.

As the businessman barreled toward Washington, he rarely used speechwriters, showing a clear preference for banter with the voters over teleprompter formality. While legions of speechwriters and wordsmiths foundered under his political opponents' banners, painting pretty yet bland pictures in the style that had worked for decades, Trump spoke plainly and trounced all of them.

The New Yorker got the message through, not just to loyal Republicans or city people, but to farmers, manufacturers, Democrats, and millions of others from all walks of life. His methods are simple and commonsense, even while breaking long-standing rules. Not only that, but they're easy to follow. And pretty fun, at that.

RULE 16: Own the Narrative (Attack, Attack, Attack)

If Donald Trump's early TV interviews seemed a bit soft-spoken or shy, it wasn't for lack of confidence. By the end of the decade, the Trump the world knows today had taken shape. Early successes, a few hard lessons, and a lot of deals had worked their magic on the young man's thinking, and one thing was clear: Donald Trump would never, ever back down from a fight.

In the introduction to his first book, Trump recalls an interview he'd seen with Tom Brokaw where the newsman had spoken with Annabel Hill, an "adorable little lady from Georgia" whose husband, a sixty-seven-year-old farmer, had taken his own life to try to get her the insurance money to save the land from the bank. It hadn't been enough, and now the bank was coming.

Trump got in contact with a vice president at the bank, asking how he could help, but was told it was too late. "Nothing or no one [was] going to stop" the auction, Trump says the banker told him. "This really got me going," he writes. "I said to the guy: 'You listen to me. If you do foreclose, I'll personally bring a lawsuit for murder against you and your bank, on the grounds that you harassed Mrs. Hill's husband to his death.'"

It changed the man from the bank's tone right quick, Trump recalls. Sure, the case sounded difficult to win, but it didn't sound like a fun fight for a bank that was already in the spotlight. "Sometimes it pays to be a little wild," Trump reminisced. And to attack, attack, attack.

It was a style Trump learned young. His father was a tough dealer, and so were the men who worked for him. When he was young, joining the guys charged with collecting late checks from people who didn't want to pay rent, they warned him to never stand in front of the door when you knocked—the guy on the other side didn't want to see you, and just might get rough.

Donald also learned from men a little less tough, but just as fearless. The lesson came in Cincinnati, on the Kentucky border, where he and his father employed a short, fat building manager named Irving. Irving was a con man, Trump quickly discovered, but the problem was this crook was the best damn building manager he could get, so he put up with him. And Trump kind of liked him, too.

One day while going door-to-door hollering at tenants who hadn't paid the rent, when Irving knocked the door was answered by a young child. This could have been the type of thing to melt Irving's cold heart, but instead he proceeded to lay into the poor kid, cursing to the young girl that she had better tell her father to pay "his f---ing rent" before Irving came back up "to knock his ass off."

Then the little girl's mother came to the door. You'd think this might finally soften Irving's heart, but she was far too pretty, and instead he hit on her until it was clear he wasn't getting anywhere. Remember: not the handsomest man hitting on a married woman whose daughter he'd just cursed at.

And then the husband came home. Young Donald was there for this scene, he writes.

"A monster" of a man, weighing at least 240 pounds, stormed into the office with "murder in his eyes," Trump recalled in *The Art of the Deal*.

"You come outside, you fat crap, I want to burn grass with you," the man said, using a threat that later became one of Trump's favorites. Donald thought his building manager was about to eat a few teeth, but Irving thought differently. Fearlessly, Irving told the man he'd be happy to throw down, but it simply wasn't legal on account of how deadly he was. The big man, who clearly would have "burned grass" with Irving—a phrase whose meaning ranges from conversational to worrisome—was apparently tamed. Angry, but he left.

The whole scene reminded the New York businessman of a tiny little lion tamer walking into a cage with a giant predator. "If that [lion] sensed any weakness or any fear, he'd destroy the trainer in a second. But instead the trainer cracks his whip, walks with authority, and, amazingly, the lion listens. Which is exactly what Irving did with this huge guy, except his whip was his mouth.

"Irving probably saved his own life," Trump continued, "just by showing no fear, and that left a very vivid impression on me. You can't be scared. You do your thing, you hold your ground, you stand up tall, and whatever happens, happens."

It's a lesson that Trump used in his career, and one he took to the campaign trail in a show that had Americans laughing out loud with approval. We hadn't seen anything like that in modern politics! He simply didn't back down. Did Bush keep us safe? Nope, Trump said. "Apologize!" the GOP pundit class demanded. No way, Trump replied.

Trump's greatest lion-taming moment on the trail came when Anderson Cooper asked him about a retweet his team had made that said Jeb Bush cared about Mexican immigration because of his wife, a Mexican woman.

(This, by the way, happens to be true, as Ann Coulter points out in her book *In Trump We Trust*. In the first two sentences of his book *Immigration Wars,* Jeb wrote, "Immigration to me is personal. It means my wife and my family.")

"Did you authorize that [retweet]?" Anderson asked on July 2015. "Do you regret that?"

"No, I didn't authorize it," Trump replied, echoing the standard political dodge we've heard for years. But then something different, addressing the second half of Anderson's question: "No, I don't regret it. I mean, you know, look, I would say that he would, if my wife were from Mexico, I think I would have a soft spot for people from Mexico. I can understand that."

But CNN wasn't done with him. Two months later, on the debate stage, Dana Bash—a "reporter" so shaken by

Hillary's defeat she started a series called "Badass Women of Washington" to make up for her loss—asked Bush, "Did Mr. Trump go too far in invoking your wife?"

"To subject my wife into the middle of a raucous political conversation was completely inappropriate," Bush challenged Trump. "And I hope you apologize for that, Donald."

"Well, I have to tell you, I hear phenomenal things," Trump replied. "I hear your wife is a lovely woman."

"She's right here," Bush said, lining Trump up for a good grass burning. "Why don't you apologize to her right now?"

But he didn't. He broke every old rule of politics, and he didn't.

"I won't do that because I said nothing wrong," he said. "She's a lovely woman."

Bush didn't double down on demanding an apology to his wife, who was present, but instead retreated to painting a positive picture of the America—and the immigration system—he envisioned. Didn't work. Bush's attack failed, and instead of looking tough he'd been publicly humiliated.

"With all of the problems, [immigration] is not an 'act of love,'" Trump said, turning to the offense. "He's weak on immigration."

"Attack, attack, attack. Never Defend," Roger Stone is fond of saying in one of his "Stone's Rules."

Bush was hardly the only victim of Trump's relentless aggression.

"Look at that face!" he exclaimed to the aging hippies

at *Rolling Stone* while watching Carly Fiorina in a debate. "Would anyone vote for that? Can you imagine that, the face of our next president?"

The media freaked out. How dare he!

Scott Adams, the *Dilbert* cartoonist who predicted Trump would win early in the process, laughed off the anguish and called it "a kill shot."

"A kill shot," he explained on his blog, "is designed with one necessary element to distinguish it from a mere insult. The kill shot has to put words to what you were already thinking in a vague sense. If you disagree with the main idea in the linguistic kill shot, it has no power. Trump only picks kill shots you agree with on some visceral level."

"Jeb Bush," Adams observed, "does look 'low energy.' We agree as soon as Trump says it, even if we had never had a concrete thought about it until he voiced it."

"Ben Carson," he continued, "does seem 'too nice' for the difficult job of staring down foreign leaders. We agree."

Trump's strategy was to show no fear. Then strike, and strike hard. Or "burn grass," if you're feeling colloquial.

In the lives the rest of us lead, far from the Reagan Library debate stage, it's far too common for people to demand something they don't deserve; to criticize you for something you haven't earned the blame for; or, as in the case of Irving, to come at you for something you absolutely deserve. In all of the above, it is essential to show no fear.

That doesn't mean don't back down when your husband

or wife demands it. Sometimes, we need to make that call even when we're supersure we're totally right. But in the arena, your declarations are going to come under attack. That, you can't change: It's how you react that will make all the difference.

"If you're right," Trump wrote in the late 1980s, "you've got to take a stand, or people will walk all over you."

Step 1 is to stand your ground. Step 2: Take their ground from them.

RULE 17: Redefine Things on Your Terms

Since he first emerged onto the political scene, everyone with a microphone or a pen has worked to define Donald Trump: who he is, what he stands for, what he wants, what he means.

Growing up, my friend Alex Pavlik had a copy of a July 1990 edition of *Heavy Metal* magazine, including a short comic called "The Wall," which featured a greedy Trump fighting another rich guy for control of New York City. It was a dark and twisted future, with Trump leading the law-and-order poor in a war on other poor. I remember it so vividly I was able to pull it back up and buy a copy on eBay with a quick Google search.

Saturday Night Live has been commenting on the highs and lows of Donald Trump since 1988, with a hysterically funny Phil Hartman making Trump's Christmas debut for him. (The show was even witty, way back then.)

The Simpsons tried their hand, too, depicting a moderately funny future where everyone's least favorite character, Lisa Simpson, was a president trying to clean up after her predecessor—one President Donald J. Trump.

In other words, Trump hasn't simply been comedy fodder for decades: The very specific character of President Donald J. Trump has been a big joke for decades. And in spite of all that, Trump became president.

It takes a lot to spurn the best satirists in America, but Trump did it, mainly by defining himself—on his buildings, through his show, on his courses, in his books, and just about everywhere else.

Of course, most of us lack the billions of dollars that enable this level of self-exposure. But all of us have the ability to be vocal, make our own style, cut our own paths before someone decides what you're going to do for you.

And that is the first thing your opponents will try to do, through gossip, asides, and other types of innuendo disguised as advice. A reputation might not be a fair thing, per se, but it's certainly a representative for you and, often, a representative in the room when you aren't anywhere nearby to defend it.

It's not a new thing, of course. Men and women have been at the mercy of their reputations for all collective memory. Every election cycle, pundits and politicians pretend to yearn for a day when civility reigned in politics, but if they ever bothered to crack open a history book (or any book, for that matter), they'd learn that politics has never been civil.

In the election of 1800, Thomas Jefferson hired James Callendar, a newspaper hit man, to go after his opponent, John Adams. Callendar did his job with vigor, labeling Adams a "hideous hermaphroditical character, which has neither the force and firmness of a man, nor the gentleness and sensibility of a woman."

"Crooked Hillary" has nothing on "Hideous Hermaphroditical John."

Callendar's turn-of-the-century trash talk added a little color, but Jefferson didn't win with simple insults. Instead, his most effective attack was labeling Adams as a warmonger, determined to wage war on France, a superpower that was wrapping up a decade of murderous revolution. The incentive to define your opponent, Jefferson showed, is based on the power that defining your opponent yields. While Adams waited patiently in Massachusetts for the states to make their choice, Jefferson made him a one-term president—and a playbook was written.

Take a look at Democratic attacks on Republican candidates. These days, they typically hit one or more of three big points: The candidate is out of touch, a warmonger, or stupid. Bob Dole was out of touch. John McCain was a warmonger. George W. Bush was a stupid warmonger. Mitt Romney . . . the list goes on.

His opponents didn't have any trouble making fun of

Donald Trump for allegedly being all three of these things, plus a racist, but he still beat them. Sure, they started in the 1980s, but from his first interview, when he was asked about real estate and he replied that he has "a great faith in New York," Donald Trump has defined the terms.

In an iconic scene of *The Godfather,* Michael Corleone tells his angry girlfriend his father was "no different than any powerful man . . . like a president or senator."

"Do you know how naive you sound, Michael?" she replies. "Presidents and senators don't have men killed!"

"Oh," Corleone quietly asks, "who's being naive, Kay?"

Al Pacino was being literal, but in politics every day, politicians rely on "attack dogs" to kill their opponents, while the person up for office stands above the fray, painting an uplifting picture of a lovely future. Not Trump. While he says he didn't care much for rolling with his dad's crews collecting late rent, Trump revels in the dirty work of politics, personally attacking and abusing opponents any chance he gets. Attacking one's opponent may seem like the most obvious tactic imaginable in politics, yet Trump took this obvious approach to such an extreme he revolutionized the political scene.

Trump grew most infamous on the trail for his unconventional, vicious, yet undeniably effective attacks. The kind that caused everyone in media and politics to assume he'd finally gone too far. And these weren't the type of attacks that everyone knew but just wouldn't say—they were whole new veins of thinking.

John McCain—the admiral's son who was tortured by the communists and refused to break—was no hero, Trump claimed. "I like people who weren't captured," he said.

Ben Carson, the famous Johns Hopkins neurosurgeon who has written whole books on his religion, might not be such a great doctor, Trump said. Maybe not so religious, Trump implied. He might even be a psychopath, the New Yorker said. "It's in the book that he's got a pathological temper," Trump told CNN's Erin Burnett. "That's a big problem because you don't cure that."

Agree with his politics or not, John McCain is, of course, an American hero. And Dr. Carson is, of course, a gifted doctor with strong religious beliefs. But Trump was willing to attack. And then there are the attacks that, well, struck a few folks as true.

The most famously effective was "low-energy Jeb." It didn't really matter that Jeb Bush's campaign said he used to prefer climbing the stairs of the Florida skyscraper capitol complex, or that Trump had taken an escalator to his own announcement party—the phrase stuck, and after that, nearly everything Jeb! did was defined through this lens Trump had set.

"Little Marco" was another. The truth is the Florida senator isn't too tall. He even got lambasted for wearing fancy, heeled boots. On top of his height, "little" evokes childishness, and Rubio, who was only forty-four in 2015, was full of youthful exuberance. "Little Marco" stuck.

When Rand Paul tried to hit back, Trump simply pointed out where he stood on the stage—the far end. "First of all, Rand Paul shouldn't even be on this stage," Trump said. "He's got one percent in the polls."

Or Ted Cruz—the leader of a tea-party grassroots movement that the billionaire described as an elitist. He called him "Lying Ted," enforcing a guttural feeling the guy couldn't be trusted. He made it stick.

It was during the general election against Hillary Clinton that Donald Trump weaponized this technique.

Trump's weaknesses were clear to the Clintons. He'd had a rocky history with women; he had skeletons in the closet; he'd given to all parties and often, it appeared, in search of influential friends. Really, on paper he was a Democrat's dream opponent. The kind of businessman they just loved to tar down and feather up.

It's obvious they assumed it would be easy. They didn't even call off the victory fireworks until just before Election Day, and even then, Hillary's friends in the media expected an easy win.

But Trump played a card no one else anywhere near his level of political status had played since the 1990s: He turned the past on the Clintons, and he defined who they were.

For years, the Clintons had deflected Republican criticism

by denying, saying it was a vast right-wing conspiracy, or saying it was "old news." Right off the bat, Donald nicknamed her "Crooked Hillary." "He can say whatever he wants to say about me, I really could care less," Clinton replied on ABC, but it was the beginning of a long campaign to paint the Clintons as corrupt—one that worked. By September, more than half the country thought she couldn't be trusted.

"The Clintons are the sordid past," he told a New Hampshire rally in late September. "We will be the bright and very clean future."

During the primaries, when people hinted at Trump's vulnerabilities, he assured the world that if the Clintons hit him, he'd hit back harder. And then after the first debate, which the press thought Clinton won, he changed his tune.

"When she hit me at the end with the women, I was going to hit her with her husband's women and I decided I shouldn't do it because her daughter was in the room," he told *Fox & Friends*. Next time, he promised, he would "hit harder." And hit harder he did.

Clinton was unfazed. "He can run his campaign however he chooses," she told reporters. "I will continue to talk about what I want to do for the American people."

After tape of him making lewd comments threatened to define him as a sexual predator, he went full tilt to turn it on his opponent.

"If you look at Bill Clinton, far worse," he said on the debate stage October 10. "Mine are words, and his was action.

His was—what he's done to women—there's never been anyone in the history of politics in this nation that's been so abusive to women. So you can say any way you want to say it, but Bill Clinton was abusive to women."

"Hillary Clinton attacked those same women and attacked them viciously," he continued, standing just feet from Hillary and with Bill in the audience.

"Four of them are here tonight," he said, referencing the accusers he'd brought into the debate audience to add to his point.

"I think it's disgraceful and I think she should be ashamed of herself, if you want to know the truth."

The audience—or the Republican part of it—applauded.

Hillary was left just denying.

Throughout the final months of the campaign, Donald Trump refused to cede an inch of ground to Democratic attacks.

"Well, I think it's terrible," he said when asked about Clinton's position on abortion. "If you go with what Hillary is saying, in the ninth month you can take the baby and rip the baby out of the womb of the mother just prior to the birth of the baby.

"And you can say that's okay and Hillary can say that's okay, but it's not okay with me," he continued. "Because based on what she's saying and based on where she's going and where she's been, you can take the baby and rip the baby out of the womb in the ninth month—on the final day—and that's not acceptable."

Republicans had spent years trying to hide from their abortion positions, terrified that Democrats would brand them as "radical" or "anti-woman." Trump, who was publicly pro-choice for decades, made a stronger defense of a pro-life position than any of them.

To Trump, Clinton was the abortionist, the enabler, the liar whose husband was a rapist—a woman who'd be in jail if the law had been followed.

Barack Obama may have beaten her once before. And Bernie Sanders did a lot of damage. But Donald Trump defined her so thoroughly as the enemy that a tepid GOP base was converted: We must vote against Clinton.

Trump also kept an incredible amount of control over his own narrative, pushing attacks off quickly. Of course the Clintons were at my wedding, I'm very powerful! Everyone is jealous because I'm a great businessman! Of course I can win the general election, I win all the time!

Define yourself in business and at home. Control your reputation. Live how you need and speak your truth loudly and speak it clearly. And when someone comes at you, make sure everyone knows what they are and what they're doing.

Hopefully life won't bring the drama of national televised debate to your doorstep (unless that's your thing, in which case good luck), but the rules work in your life as well: Define yourself. Define your opponents. Control the world. Or at least your own world.

And if you need to deal with journalists, I'm sorry. Here's how you can use them.

RULE 18: Journalists Are Tools. Use Them.

Howard Segermark, a notorious D.C. mover and groover, once asked the classic conservative journalist M. Stanton "Stan" Evans if it was legal to shoot a reporter.

Stan thought about this for a moment, then nodded authoritatively and pronounced, "Yes. If he's got his pen and pad, you can consider him armed and dangerous."

Journalists can be dangerous. They can be demanding. A fair number of them are evil.

But perhaps the most common trait among journalists is that we are lazy. Very, very lazy. And not a small number of reporters are not nearly as bright as they fancy themselves.

Sure, we all dream of the big scoop, the recognition it comes with, the power and the glory, but it's a hard job that doesn't pay so well, and the reality is, it's easy to mail it in. The greatest temptation of all is the temptation to publish a big scoop we've heard simply on its face. And when you combine this temptation with the always-be-posting pressures of a digital newsroom, well, it's easy for a mindful person to craft the news.

When Trump was working on his Television City

project—a major New York development—he held a news conference to explain the details and nuances and traffic impact and the rest to reporters. Turned out, they didn't care—they just wanted to know about the fantastical claim he'd made: Donald Trump said he was going to build the world's tallest building.

The building was never built, but the press on the plan was immediate. The news made the front page of the *New York Times,* made the evening news, made *Newsweek,* which still mattered back then. Everyone was interested.

Trump pretended to be surprised by this in his recollection, but it's a bit of a stretch. For years, he'd been working with the press both as himself and, when he felt it was required, posing as a spokesman for himself.

"John Miller" and "John Barron" were two of his favorite monikers. The first known times Trump assumed one of these aliases to dial a reporter and dish on himself was 1980. "Some reporters found the calls from Miller or Barron disturbing or even creepy; others thought they were just examples of Trump being playful," the *Washington Post* reported in a 2016 write-up.

"I'm not saying that they necessarily like me," Trump admitted of reporters in 1987. "Sometimes they write positively, and sometimes they write negatively. But from a pure business point of view, the benefits of being written about have far outweighed the drawbacks."

And he lived this, with the *Post* reporting nearly thirty

years later, "He made himself available to reporters at nearly any time, for hours on end. And he called them, too, to promote his own projects, but also with juicy bits of gossip."

Trump didn't change his habits as chief executive.

In his first ninety-nine days in office, The Donald was seemingly constantly available to the press—even while bashing it on a near-daily basis. In addition to the 145 speeches and remarks he gave, an analysis by CBS shows, Trump gave one solo news conference, eight news conferences with leaders from around the world, nine interviews to Fox News, and twenty-three interviews to other outlets—figures about on par with his similarly media-hungry predecessor.

Jonathan Swan of Axios summed up Trump's style with journalists well: It wasn't simply confrontational, despite the apocalyptic and shrieking whines of the vast majority of the coastal press elite. In his long relationship with the press, Donald Trump picked up a thing or three.

One, Swan wrote in "How Trump Thinks Like a Journalist," was that reporters love to break news. "I'm giving you something first," he told Bloomberg in one interview. "We have breaking news," he told another reporter during a different interview.

"One thing I've learned about the press," Trump wrote in the 1980s, "is that they're always hungry for a good story, and the more sensational the better. It's the nature of the job and I understand that."

Trump's second weapon, Swan writes, is flattery. When

being interviewed by a journalist, Trump loves to cite their prior work. "You reported this once," he told an interviewer. (Hint: Even if someone doesn't like the president, they like to hear he notices their work.)

When he came upon us in that New Hampshire steakhouse, his flattery of our friend at the table was over-the-top and hysterical. Heck, we all knew it wasn't remotely true, but that didn't stop the guy from blushing a little, if somewhat out of embarrassment. It will be a long-distant day he forgets those compliments from the future president.

A third thing Trump learned is an old one for press flacks of all kind: playing the reporter's boss, telling them to publish different graphics with their stories, saying which angles he feels haven't been properly covered and the like.

It's not that these are so unusual in Washington—it's that these are unusual characteristics in the president of the United States. Certainly, these are not unprecedented, though. Long before dozens of reporters formed a guild to wrestle their way into their own rooms in the White House, Franklin Delano Roosevelt would hold frequent meetings with the reporters from the most important outlets in the country.

During the meetings, the reporters would get to sit with him in the Oval Office, where he'd ask them what they wanted to talk about that day. When they sourced him, they often had to cite a White House "source" with knowledge of the situation.

And like Trump, FDR loved to go around the press, holding his famous fireside chats to speak directly to the American people. We're a far cry from those warm, nostalgic memories, but in his first one hundred days, Trump reached right around the media translators to tweet at the American people 518 times (though he deleted 11).

The press can play St. Obama and the Devil Named Trump all day, but it's difficult to get in between the president and his audience when he tweets, say, "I don't know Putin, have no deals in Russia, and the haters are going crazy - yet Obama can make a deal with Iran, #1 in terror, no problem!"

Or, "As families prepare for summer vacations in our National Parks - Democrats threaten to close them and shut down the government. Terrible!"

Those last two messages alone received nearly 66,000 retweets and more than 249,000 likes on the social media platform.

Trump learned early in his career that it is earned media that is the best kind of media. There's simply no way advertising can beat it—even when it's "bad press." Every story the *Times* wrote criticizing decisions he made while building Trump Tower, for example, included mention that it was going to be one of the most luxurious buildings in the city.

"It's really quite simple," he explains. "If I take a full-page ad in the *New York Times* to publicize a project, it might cost $40,000, and in any case, people tend to be skeptical about advertising. But if *the New York Times* writes even a moderately positive one-column story about one of my deals, it doesn't cost me anything, and it's worth a lot more than $40,000."

When he announced his candidacy for president, he said he was going to self-fund. That didn't end up coming to pass quite the way he said it, but if you look at how he earned his media, it might as well have.

In the primaries, Jeb Bush, Ben Carson, Marco Rubio, and Ted Cruz spent more than Trump had (when they dropped out, comparatively) with half the coverage. In the general election, Clinton raised $75 million more than the winner. And yet, Quantcast calculated Trump had earned $4.96 billion in media he didn't pay for. Clinton, the first woman to be on a major party's presidential ticket, by contrast, earned $3.24 billion.

"The only thing worse in politics than being wrong," Roger Stone rattles off in another of his "Stone's Rules," "is being boring."

When Trump took the stage during rallies, one campaign trail reporter told me, he knew when the cameras were live by a light that would turn on. If the light came on, he'd immediately start riffing in an effort to capture the news cycle. No light? No show.

And it wasn't even all politics all day. His staying power over decades of saturation coverage isn't based simply on his ability to comment on matters of business and real estate. Anything interesting to the media was Trump's domain, from business to politics to Hollywood love lives.

"Robert Pattinson should not take back Kristen Stewart," he tweeted in October 2012. "She cheated on him like a dog & will do it again—just watch. He can do much better!"

Reporters are not your friend, Trump learned quickly enough, but that doesn't mean you can't use them to your advantage. Through stories, scoops, quotes, tweets, calls, and appearances, Donald Trump manipulated so much coverage that angry journalists lashed out at CNN's Jeff Zucker and wrote cringe-worthy "confessions" in major papers.

How could they let this happen, they wondered. Why didn't they do more to stop Trump, they asked. It was amazing to watch, too. And the best part is none of their egos left room for the simplest answer: Donald Trump outsmarted them.

And there was never a week of media that Donald Trump controlled more closely than the one when Republican Senator Mitch McConnell failed to get Obamacare repeal to the finish line.

The Senate majority leader had promised a vote by June 30, when lawmakers headed home to their constituents for the Independence Day break.

The press knew it was a hard fight for Trump and McConnell. For months, Republican politicians had rassled and wrangled, with the conservative, liberal, and business wings of the party taking shot after shot at each other. Democrats, unsurprisingly, had promised early on that they would never help the GOP repeal their bill, and from the sideline, they hurled stones across the aisle and loudly asked why they weren't being consulted.

Most members of the press knew, of course, that the Democrats' offers were disingenuous and the Republicans' mission difficult, but they took too much joy in criticizing the president to pay that any mind. After months of predicting failure by Speaker of the House Paul Ryan—and, later, Mitch McConnell—their excitement was electric.

"Senators are being told it's not possible to just let Obamacare fail—that if the Better Care bill fails, Rs will have to work with Ds *(horrors!)* later this year to help shore up the exchanges," Axios's Mike Allen wrote on June 27.

"Forget passage for the moment," *Politico* Playbook's reporters wrote that same morning. "Republicans have not yet secured the votes to begin work on the bill. It'll be a crazy week. And make no mistake: Republicans might not be able to repeal and replace Obamacare. The situation is that dire for them."

That morning, across the river from *Politico*'s offices, in Washington, D.C., three principals, by one Senate communications aide's guess, already knew for sure that the GOP was going to have to postpone the vote. Those three were Mitch McConnell, possibly John Cornyn, who was in charge of tallying the votes, and President Donald Trump.

At 9:30 a.m., Trump's Twitter account erupted.

"Fake News CNN," he wrote, "is looking at big management changes now that they got caught falsely pushing their phony Russian stories. Ratings way down!"

Seventeen minutes later, another volley: "So they caught Fake News CNN cold, but what about NBC, CBS & ABC? What about the failing @nytimes & @washingtonpost? They are all Fake News!"

And then, for nine hours, his account went silent. In those nine hours, the press went wild. While they briefly broke to cover McConnell's announcement that the vote would be postponed till after the July 4 recess, the story of the day on every network was Trump's attacks on the media. Sure, America's health care was important, but in the minds of D.C. journalists, nothing is more important than themselves. And Donald Trump had disrespected that.

Two days later, as the Senate prepared to leave the city for yet another vacation without their top legislative priority accomplished, the party once again faced a pounding narrative in the press.

Starting at 9:52 in the morning, Trump tweeted, "I heard poorly rated @Morning_Joe speaks badly of me (don't watch anymore). Then how come low I.Q. Crazy Mika, along with Psycho Joe, came . . . to Mar-a-Lago 3 nights in a row around New Year's Eve, and insisted on joining me. She was bleeding badly from a face-lift. I said no!"

Living in Washington, D.C., you'd be forgiven for thinking that by attacking a powerful and famous woman with a broad media platform for her cosmetic surgery, he'd sacrificed an innocent child on the altar of Cthulhu.

As the world held its breath the next morning, Joe Scarborough and Mika Brzezinski postponed their vacation plans to respond live on their TV show (we know the details because MSNBC teased this for twenty-four hours). Mika's column explaining, in quite a bit of detail, that her mom said she needed "a chin tweak" was the talk of the town. From CNN to Fox to MSNBC, the feeling was universal: This kind of talk by the president of the United States was highly not okay.

No conversation, from the television to the bar, spent more than an obligatory minute on the Republicans as they sulked home in failure. It was "The Donald Trump Show," and it was twenty-four hours.

"We weren't getting anything from Senate leadership," one of the Republican staffers tasked with the party's messaging told me as the week wrapped up. "We had no idea. But [the press] didn't come. They didn't even care."

"It was one of two things," he continued. "It was either Donald Trump's PR genius, or divine intervention."

"Which one?" he challenged, over the glass of bourbon that signaled the end of a long week and the beginning of July's short recess. "You tell me."

We're not all dealing with reporters. For most Americans, it's either an exceptionally good or bad day when reporters are asking around. But there plenty of people—managers, associates, competitors—who act the same, gathering intelligence, spreading it, and either making or frustrating your plans.

It will be necessary to run right at them, from time to time, but never lose track of the ability to manipulate instead. If you're clumsy, they'll know and be annoyed as heck (like some of the reporters talking to "John Miller"), but if you're smart about it, you can once again define the message.

Just don't get convoluted—keep it simple.

RULE 19: Keep Your Message Simple

Donald Trump's opponents didn't think he was so smart, though. Most of them didn't until it was too late. Even after he outsmarted them and beat them, a large number of them couldn't come to terms with it.

Despite the hand-wringing over Russia, the Daily Caller News Foundation's Blake Neff wrote that the Clinton campaign can't blame Kremlin hackers for their candidate saying she wanted "to put a lot of coal miners and coal companies out of business"—something she actually said in a March 2016 Democratic debate.

Nor, he adds, did Putin's men hack her campaign trail plan to reroute her plane from Milwaukee (where she should have been campaigning) to Phoenix (where her campaign admitted it was attempting to run up the score).

Nor, he says, did any Russian spy implant "electrodes on

an unsuspecting Clinton's neck as she [took] a nap, causing her to later bark like a dog during a rally in Reno, Nevada."

She—not Vladimir Putin—simply ran a terrible campaign.

The FBI's James Comey is the reason Clinton lost, they claim, thereby literally blaming the cops for getting busted for breaking the law after decades of operating as if it didn't apply to her family. It turned out Comey had to bring it back up because the first time, he'd just decided that he wasn't going to prosecute, despite a mountain of evidence pointing toward moving forward. The Democrats would be back to his side later, of course, when it was helpful to do so.

Can't be too, too harsh on Comey here, of course—for decades the law hadn't applied to the Clinton family. It's just that it isn't the former FBI director's "fault" for investigating her misdeeds.

Oh, and then there's that America hates women (if you listen to a lot of activists and politicians). "Misogyny" is the term for it, and she said in a May 2017 interview that she's writing a book on it now. It's an easy excuse to make, until you decide to check if it's at all accurate. Two professors tasked themselves with proving that when the roles were reversed, with Trump played by a woman and Clinton by a man, the audience would back the man.

"We both thought that the inversion would confirm our liberal assumption—that no one would have accepted Trump's behavior from a woman, and that the male Clinton would seem like the much stronger candidate," said the male performer, described by New York University as a specialist in "ethnodrama." "But we kept checking in with each other and realized that this disruption—a major change in perception—was happening."

The audience, it turned out after two performances, found Hillary even less likable as a man.

Indeed, Donald Trump's opponents have spent almost all of the time looking outward, and rarely inward. The idea that he outmessaged them has barely occurred to a lot of the folks who mock him.

"They're sending us not the right people," Trump begins in a video clip on the site of the overwhelmingly self-satisfied *New York* magazine. The overwhelmingly self-satisfied caption reads, "Donald J. Trump has the grammar of an 11-year-old. That's not opinion. That's research-proven."

"Donald Trump might have trouble if he ever appears on 'Are you smarter than a fifth grader?'" declared an article by Mashable, a significantly less self-serious social media blog with a liberal bent.

Both articles were based on research published by Carnegie Mellon University. A study by the predictably liberal and always near-broke *Boston Globe* was even harsher, reporting, "with his own choice of words and his short, simple sentences, Trump's speech could have been comprehended by a fourth-grader. Yes, a fourth-grader."

Politico magazine demoted Trump even further, pegging his grammar at a third-grade level based on a single speaking appearance. "It's obvious that Trump's verbal deficit, as grating as it may be on the ears of the educated class," the reporter complained, "has not caused him much political pain."

"Donald Trump isn't a simpleton," he generously offered; "he just talks like one. If you were to market Donald Trump's vocabulary as a toy, it would resemble a small box of Lincoln Logs."

To their credit, some in the media seemed to realize Trump's style had an incredible appeal.

One *Washington Post* article by a "freelance writer and communications consultant" was titled "Donald Trump speaks like a sixth-grader. All politicians should." "A presidential candidate wants to be understood by all voters, from immigrants whose first language isn't English to those with advanced degrees in linguistics," she wrote. "Trump rarely uses speechwriters, yet he's grasped one of their principles: It is more important to be understood than to use $10 words."

"Donald Trump connects with voters by using simple, commanding language that even a fourth-grader could understand, a report says—and the style has been so successful that his competitors are copying it," reported the pro-Trump *New York Post*.

In a story in *Wired*—the first magazine I've ever seen that bragged about letting a politician, one Barack Obama, edit their content—the writer conceded, "At this point in the Republican presidential primary race, Donald Trump's intelligence is tough to dispute," adding, "To his supporters, Trump's style is refreshingly direct."

Washington, D.C., is a town where you can make a career as a fancy-talking speechwriter. The *Wall Street Journal*'s Peggy Noonan first gained notice for penning Ronald Reagan's "Challenger speech" (though the most memorable line was a quote from an American pilot) and later cemented her chops with H. W. Bush's "thousand points of light" line. She parlayed this fame into a column at the *Wall Street Journal*, which won her a Pulitzer in 2017. It's a town where there are so many Republican speechwriters retired from the White House that they have teamed up to found their own consulting company, the White House Writers Group.

And it's a town Donald Trump has little use for. While major addresses, like his inaugural or major foreign policy addresses, are written by people like aide Stephen Miller and others, CBS found that more than 80 percent of the speeches and remarks he made in his first one hundred days in office had no teleprompter notes to read from.

It's a tough way for his staff to keep up, but it's crucial to his appeal with a large number of his supporters. Words and phrases like "sad," "bad," "winning," "terrible," "big league," "the greatest," and "very, very good" are common in his speech, "OK?" It's not hard to get, even when it's hard to follow in print.

Sure, Donald Trump speaks simply. And Donald Trump is "very, very" straightforward.

I'm rich and I mean business, he has declared for years. When quizzed on why he might be a good presidential candidate in 2011 by a skeptical *Good Morning America,* Trump said, "Part of the beauty of me is that I am very rich."

"I have built an incredible company and have accumulated one of the greatest portfolios of real estate assets, many of which are considered to be among the finest and most iconic properties in the world," he said in 2016. "This is the kind of thinking the country needs.

"I deal with foreign countries," he said, hitting on foreign policy and his business acumen at the same time. "I made a lot of money dealing against China. I've made a lot of money dealing against many other countries."

America is in trouble, he's said for years. Deep trouble. And everyone knows it.

"They laugh at us," he told Larry King in 1987, citing the Gulf oil states and Japanese trade practices. "Behind our backs, they laugh at us because of our own stupidity."

"It's time to reject the political and media elite that's bled our country dry," Trump said nearly three decades later in Florida as Election Day drew near. "Our country is a laughingstock," he added later in the speech. "All over the world, they're laughing."

He even called his campaign book *Crippled America,* before changing the message to *Great Again* after winning the election. Buy that book, by the way; it's published by the good guys.

A favorite is a speech he made as president: "We never win and we don't fight to win," he told a room full of governors. "We don't fight to win. We've either got to win or don't fight it at all."

The press flipped out that he was attacking our fighting men and women, but any American with a brain and a heart knew he was right—and he wasn't attacking our servicemen, he was attacking the politicians tying their hands and unwilling to let them unleash the hell our enemies no longer feared like they ought to.

Similarly, Trump said something most of the other politicians had been afraid to say, and in simple terms: Foreign countries are sending their worst, not their best.

"We have some bad, bad people in the country, and we're going to get them out," he said in one of the many iconic moments of the final debate. "We have some bad hombres and we're going to get them out."

Once again, the media freaked out, but a lot of voters knew it was true.

He even once bragged about screwing Libyan dictator Muammar Gaddafi. "He paid me more for one night than the land was worth for two years, and then I didn't let him use the land," Trump said. "That's what we should be doing. I don't want to use the word 'screwed,' but I screwed him."

On his opponents, the simplicity and straightforward nature of his attacks shine brightest.

"I think the only difference between me and the other candidates," he told the *New York Times* in 1999 while considering a run for the White House, "is that I'm more honest and my women are more beautiful."

"I know words," he told a South Carolina rally sixteen years later. "I have the best words. I have the best, but there is no better word than 'stupid.'"

He'd been talking about President Obama, a man who, like him or not, is hard to call straight-up stupid.

But in addition to simplicity, Trump has never been one to avoid a little hyperbole.

"People want to believe something is the biggest and the greatest and the most spectacular," he wrote in *The Art of the Deal*. "I call it truthful hyperbole. It's an innocent form of exaggeration—and a very effective form of promotion."

Why? Simple: "People may not always think big themselves, but they can still get very excited by those who do."

That's why, in the right situation, don't be afraid to use hyperbole. Don't lie—just paint a bright picture on where you want to be; use bold colors. The city (or house) on the hill is a fine thing to aim for, even if step one is getting out of the basement apartment.

"Our people look for a cause to believe in," Governor Ronald Reagan told conservatives gathered in a D.C. hotel in 1975. "Is it a third party we need, or is it a new and revitalized second party, raising a banner of no pale pastels, but bold colors which make it unmistakably clear where we stand on all of the issues troubling the people?"

He knew the troubles of governing would be more complicated than that, but he didn't hesitate one moment to raise the banner.

The real thing to be afraid of is people—be it voters, bosses, colleagues, your wife, the kids—not understanding where you're coming from. And simplicity in communication is the key in all its forms.

America's most famous socialist writer, Ernest Hemingway, reached the whole country with his visions of heroism, sacrifice, human nature, and human longing with prose so simple a child can read them—even if that child can't yet grasp their depth.

Obama was inexplicably revered for his astounding oratory. Chris Matthews is rightly panned for feeling "this thrill go up my leg" when he spoke, but so apparently impressive was Obama's presence, the *New York Times'* "conservative" columnist David Brooks told the nearly forgotten *New Republic* magazine, "I was looking at his pant leg and his perfectly creased pant, and I'm thinking, a) He's going to be president and b) He'll be a very good president."

David Brooks is a leading public intellectual, born in Canada, raised in Manhattan, residing in D.C., and married to a woman seven years older than his son, and his point shines through. "I divide people," he told the *New Republic,* "into people who talk like us and who don't talk like us."

For all the fancy words, it's an entertaining exercise to ask Obamaphiles what his most famous speech is. If they actually have an answer, ask for their favorite line in it. If they have a line they can recall, give them a quarter. If they don't, they're like the vast majority of Obamaphiles: They basked in his warmth but can't really recall what he said.

Contrast that with Trump, whose simple words aren't called great by folks "who talk like" David Brooks, but cut through the swampy air.

There's a time for big words: on Inauguration Day, during solemn and formal speeches. But not every day.

When you're trying to paint your picture, fly your banner, or just get your point across to your family and friends, be understood.

Be simple, be straightforward, be understood, and get your allies on board. If you do something of worth, you'll have haters and critics no matter your cause. There will be colleagues who hate you, or your teenage kid will scream you aren't their real parent. If you're public, there will be sore losers in the press. When you're winning, you can deal with them later.

5

★

Dealing with Critics
(and Other Haters and Losers)

On April 27, 2011, the most powerful man in the world publicly released his long-form birth certificate, telling reporters at the White House, "We do not have time for this kind of silliness."

A quick 490 miles up the road, Donald Trump's helicopter landed by a hangar of journalists, cameramen, and flashing lights. They—the press—were not too impressed with Mr. Trump. At least not as impressed as he was with himself.

"You ready?" he asked the reporters, scanning the television cameras to see which ones were playing him live and ignoring the questions from the newspaper writers. "Whenever you get ready, I'm okay."

"Good morning," he began, once the cable hosts in New York had quieted down.

It was time for the reckoning, the reporters thought.

Sure, a young Barack Obama—or the literary agent representing him—had begun the rumors he was born in Kenya in a pamphlet promoting his work. Yes, Hillary Clinton—or her campaign—had spread the word he was a Kenyan during a vicious Democratic primary battle. But Donald Trump—the reality TV star no one "respectable" took seriously—had built a Republican presidential primary campaign out of the missing birth certificate. And never mind the Hillary, it was time for Donald Trump to suffer, the reporters were certain.

"Today, I'm very proud of myself," he began, causing my then-small newsroom in Manassas, Virginia, to burst into uproarious laughter. "Because I've accomplished something that nobody else has been able to accomplish. I was just informed, while on the helicopter, that our president has finally released a birth certificate.

"I want to look at it, but I hope it's true so we can get on to much more import matters—so the press can stop asking me questions," he said, subtly and quickly flipping the narrative.

"He should have done it a long time ago," he said next, turning the onus onto the president.

"Why he didn't do it when the Clintons asked for it," he wondered, pointing to Hillary. "Why he didn't do it when everybody else was asking for it," he wondered, pointing at the country, "I don't know. But I am really honored in playing such a big role in hopefully—hopefully—getting rid of this issue.

"I am really proud, I am really honored," he said moments before furious reporters began peppering him with questions. "Now we can talk about oil, we can talk about gasoline prices, we can talk about China ripping off this country, we can talk about OPEC doing numbers on us like no one has ever done before—we can talk about issues.

"So I feel I've accomplished something really, really important, and I'm honored by it.

"I'm taking great credit."

RULE 20: Life Is War

Fifty-two weeks later, Donald and Melania Trump waved to a crowd of tourists, aides, and actors in Trump Tower before taking an escalator ride downstairs to announce his candidacy for the Republican presidential nomination.

Neil Young's "Rockin' in the Free World" was blasting—a song the old hippie had written in 1989 attacking George H. W. Bush one month into his new presidency.

"We've got a thousand points of light," Young sang, echoing a speech Peggy Noonan had helped write, "for the homeless man. We got a kinder, gentler machine-gun hand." (The kind of hand I always thought would be cool to have.)

Like any of the varied music Trump would play at his rallies over the next seventeen months, he probably just picked it because he liked it, but the dig at Dad likely didn't sit well with the media-anointed Republican front-runner, Jeb Bush.

Jeb! had announced his own candidacy the day prior to Trump.

A *Time* article was titled "How Donald Trump Stole Jeb Bush's Moment," but it wasn't a nice piece. "Despite America's pleas, Trump insists on being Trump. I suppose we should not be surprised by this," the columnist wrote, citing his own tweet "begging" Trump not to run.

That didn't matter to Donald Trump, though. He'd started his campaign the way he wanted to—by sucking the oxygen out of the room and steering coverage from the front-runner's big day to himself. The attacks from his competition and the media were swift and designed to cripple his fledgling campaign.

But that was nothing new—Trump has been dealing with haters his whole life. And when he went for the biggest prize in the nation, he came out swinging from the beginning. The warning was clear: If you come at The Donald, you had best not miss. Everyone missed.

People have been taking aim at Donald Trump for a long time. That's part of business, entertainment, television, politics, and success in general—all things Trump pursued. His feuds are both hysterical and well documented, particularly his long-standing battle with Rosie O'Donnell.

"When people treat me badly or unfairly or try to take advantage of me, my attitude, all my life, has been to fight back very hard," Trump wrote in the mid-1980s. "The risk is that you'll make a bad situation worse, and I certainly don't recommend this approach to everyone. But my experience is that if you're fighting for something you believe in—even if it means alienating some people along the way—things usually work out for the best in the end."

Before entering politics, Trump brought the philosophy, gaining a reputation for knock-down, drawn-out, public battles with government, competitors, entertainers.

"For years, Mr. Trump was a nearly constant source of conflict," the *Washington Post* reported on his relationship with the local Palm Beach, Florida, government. "He sought exemptions from local ordinances, bent and broke regulations, and complained about everything from the frequency of drawbridge openings—'far too often,' he wrote in a 2001 letter to transportation officials—to the 'deplorable' condition of a neighbor's loading dock."

At his golf club in Bedminster, New Jersey, the *Post* reports, he fought local government over the right to be buried there.

"They say you can't fight city hall," he wrote in 2008, "but I have no problems going against conventional wisdom."

While he bragged on the campaign trail about never settling and not caring how much it cost to fight back, the first bit is an example of classic Trump brand hyperbole—Trump settles, sometimes for better, other times for worse—but the second part is true: He will spend money to not back down.

"I'm not saying I would also have won, but if I went down, it would have been kicking and screaming," he wrote on a hostile takeover he witnessed playing out between two other companies over a hotel. "I would have closed the hotel and let it rot. That's just my makeup. I fight when I feel I'm getting screwed, even if it's costly and difficult and highly risky."

Indeed, a 2016 analysis by the little-read *USA Today* found that Trump "and his businesses have been involved in at least 3,500 legal actions in federal and state courts during the past three decades. They range from skirmishes with casino patrons to million-dollar real estate suits to personal defamation lawsuits."

"When we believe we are in the right, we are going to pursue the matter to the end," Trump attorney Alan Garten told the tabloid. "We are not going to cave to pressure."

Despite all of this, when Trump entered the political arena, the world underestimated him. Which Trump would we be getting? they wondered. Before the Trump Tower announcement, I assumed—quite wrongly—we'd get Trump the Entertainer, like it seemed we'd gotten last time around when he toyed with the idea but just kept it going awhile for fun. What I—and every jerk I know—missed at first glance is that Trump the Fighter, Trump the Entertainer, and Trump the Businessman are inseparable.

In the first primary debate, which positioned Trump and Bush at the center due to their higher polling numbers, the peripheral candidates were quick to attack the entertainer they expected would be an easy target as a former Democrat.

"He buys and sells politicians of all stripes," Senator Rand Paul whined in the opening minutes.

"Well," Trump shot back, "I've given him plenty of money."

When Megyn Kelly started listing off insults he'd used on women, Trump smiled into the microphone, "Only Rosie O'Donnell," to thunderous applause.

When she continued, he flipped it: "I think the big problem this country has is being politically correct."

Tomi Lahren, a young spitfire seemingly impervious to deep thoughts or self-reflection, nevertheless nailed Trump's performance in her review: "Fearless."

It wasn't long before Jeb, who had dodged a fight in the first round, was forced to take on the brash real estate mogul sinking him in the polls. "This is a tough business, to run for president," he sarcastically cautioned, flailing for the role of elder statesman.

"Oh, you're a tough guy, Jeb, I know," Trump laughed, to applause. "Real tough!"

"You're never going to be president of the United States by insulting your way to the presidency," Bush replied, setting up endless Internet jokes for after the election.

"Well, let's see," his target parried, "I'm at 42 [percent] and you're at 3, so so far I'm doing better.

"You know, you started off over here, Jeb," Trump continued. "You're moving over further and further. Pretty soon you're going to be off the end!"

When Jeb would fight back, Trump would cut his legs right out. "More energy tonight, I like that," he interjected to applause during one of Jeb's more energized attack attempts.

"Wrong!" he yelled over another one.

Over the course of the campaign, the guy who rode an escalator to his campaign announcement would hit Jeb! on being "a low-energy person," on his fashion, on his negotiation skills, on being "very, very weak" on immigration, on copying words like "anchor baby" that Trump had used, on his small and sleepy crowds, on Common Core, on being unhappy, on being reluctant to run, on being "another Bush."

"When somebody hits me, I'm gonna hit 'em back," he explained in an interview on his open war on Bush. And to Trump, politics was absolutely war without weapons. To Trump, in this war there were no noncombatants in the Bush clan.

Bush's brother, father: No one Jeb attempted to use to bolster his own credentials was safe from The Donald's fire—a new reality that took much of the American political world by surprise.

After President Trump attacked "low I.Q. Crazy Mika" Brzezinski and "Psycho Joe" Scarborough, the press went tattling to first lady Melania in the hope she might condemn her husband. "As the first lady has stated publicly in the past," Melania spokeswoman Stephanie Grisham replied, "when her husband gets attacked, he will punch back ten times harder."

"I don't go out of my way to be cordial to enemies," Trump mused in *The Art of the Deal*.

Throughout the battles, he used nicknames to highlight insecurities, he hit on television and in newspapers, he confronted opponents directly, and his no-holds-barred approach worked over and over again.

Modern politics hadn't seen open war like this in years. Even Lyndon B. Johnson wasn't so up-front in his devastation. The Clinton family—destroyers of worlds—were never so straightforward in their political attacks.

That doesn't mean kill your opponents. Even Trump didn't start having his opponents killed until he was president and "his opponents" were guys like old ISIS & Company. The lesson is ruthlessly defeating the people who want to beat you.

This is applicable to business and all forms of competition. It's about defeating the people who want to beat you—and only when they've made the wrong move.

Donald Trump is not known for restraint—even though, despite the popular narrative, he displays it daily. Jeb Bush and Trump got along just fine until Trump took a swipe at him. In that contest, where there would be only one winner, it was no-holds-barred war. He hit Bush, hit any family members who spoke up, cut through allegedly sacred tropes, and explained it was all because Jeb had hit him first.

His opponents have derided Trump's attacks on his most vocal critics as bullying, but the majority of his most famous and public fights show a clear line of progression: Trump is poked, Trump is sniped, Trump is hit, Trump responds with overwhelming force.

Sometimes, however, we need to strike first. It's the fastest way to win a fistfight, and it's even helpful in the court system. But Donald Trump showed that in a contest that has a clear winner and loser, the most important thing is to strike hard: harder than they ever thought you would, and hard enough to knock them down.

"I'm the first to admit that I am very competitive and that I'll do nearly anything within legal bounds to win," Trump writes. "Sometimes, part of making a deal is denigrating your competition."

But one of the lessons of the indirect warfare Trump deploys so well is that an open attack isn't always the best approach. Sometimes that's because the competition is too difficult to take on openly on any front, and sometimes it's because there's simply a better way to do it.

Why destroy an enemy you can simply outsmart?

RULE 21: The People You Do Need, You Can Outsmart

By the looks of it, the president and the press don't get along so well. They bicker and fight almost constantly.

Near the end of the September before the election, for example, the *New York Times* did its darnedest to outdo itself by publishing a very, very thinly veiled comparison of Trump to Adolf Hitler, called, "In 'Hitler,' an Ascent from 'Dunder-head' to Demagogue."

Comparing people to Hitler is lazy work, but since the author didn't use Trump's name, the praise flowed in from all parts of the media. CNN's Dylan Byers praised her cleverness for skipping on his name. *Politico*'s chief Washington correspondent retweeted Byers's praise, calling the review "the most compelling case against Trump by anyone yet." In an amazing circle of pleasure, Byers then quoted *Politico*'s guy tweeting Byers in a CNN story about the review. (If "the media" was a movie, it would look less like *All the President's Men* and more like a porno starring a single ugly person.)

The *Washington Post*'s book critic chimed in with, "The beauty of this . . . review is that it doesn't make the obvious point because it doesn't need to. . . ."

"The form she has chosen—perhaps even invented—gives her deniability, to be sure," gushed a senior scholar at Poynter, a self-described "global leader in journalism." He went on to compare the *New York Times*' completely unsubtle Hitler comparison to poets protesting Communist censorship in Poland or writers sneaking around authoritarian Singapore in the '90s.

The professor of journalism was actually so swept up in the romanticism of "the paper of record," comparing Trump to Hitler, the stylings conjured up images of people who really did risk life and death to critique the government. The irony—that the real risk would be supporting Donald Trump in Manhattan—barely crosses their scholarly minds.

In fact, the only time I was attacked in New York City outside of a few teenage fights was walking to the train with a group of reporters the day after Election Day. I was carrying a bunch of Trump campaign signs from the night's victory rally to hang alongside other newsroom campaign memorabilia from all across the political spectrum. I was also wearing the red hat because, honestly, ever since I wore plaid pants and spiked hair as a kid, I've enjoyed trolling random strangers.

But there was no joy in Mudville that November Wednesday, and one woman in her twenties yelled, "How can you wear that!?" before knocking my hat and glasses off my face and trying to grab our cheap cardboard souvenirs. Katie Frates, then an editor a little younger than the attacker, chased her off while I grabbed my glasses and yelled a little.

A crowd had gathered by then; a do-gooder who likely hadn't seen any of what happened was ready to throw punches my way—all in the name of New York tolerance. I met their gazes straight on, didn't move, cursed them off, and then took some cash out of the ATM so I could buy my overworked reporters a great slice of New York pizza before the train.

I'd been trolling with the hat, I admit, though physical assault and a street mob was an overreaction by any standard.

And Trump, for his part, is not entirely innocent himself. His long war trolling the press has been waged since his early days in the public eye.

"I don't think they've portrayed what I'm really all about," he worried to Mike Wallace in his first *60 Minutes* interview in 1985. "Well, I believe they like making me out to be somebody a little more sinister than I really am. And I don't look at myself necessarily as being sinister."

"I have a running war with the media," he declared at CIA headquarters more than thirty years later, in his first month as president of the United States. "They are among the most dishonest human beings on earth."

Just a few weeks later, during one of his rowdier and more entertaining televised press conferences, he took a lighter tone. "I'm changing [your nickname] from fake news, though," he informed CNN's Jim Acosta. The new name? "Very fake news." Even the haters had a good laugh.

"But aren't you concerned, sir, that you are undermining the people's faith in the First Amendment, freedom of the press, press in this country when you call stories you don't like fake news?" Acosta persisted. "Why not just call it a story you don't like?"

"If you were straight and really told it how it is . . . I would be your biggest booster," Trump replied. "I would be your biggest fan in the world."

And everyone knows that if we're being honest, he is their biggest fan in the world: Even while he's fighting this decades-long "running war," he's been happy—very happy—to use them.

In 1979, Trump was shaking hands, throwing dollars, and hustling hard to get Trump Tower built. The City Planning Commission was going to vote on his zoning soon, and he wanted to put a little pressure on them. So he called his once-friends at the *New York Times*.

"I took a calculated risk when I invited [chief *New York Times* architecture critic Ada Louise] Huxtable to look at our model and renderings before the City Planning Commission voted on our zoning," Trump wrote in his *Art of the Deal* chapter on the tower. "The power of *The New York Times* is just awesome. It is certainly one of the most influential institutions in the world, and I recognized that anything Huxtable wrote would have enormous impact."

In June, the famous lover of classic New York architecture and critic of skyscrapers came to see the plans.

On July 1, the *Times*' art section ran her piece, titled "A New York Blockbuster of Superior Design," alongside a picture of the tower that Trump hoped to build. Huxtable wasn't too keen on the size of the structure, but Trump's bet paid off when she blamed that on the city and moved on to praise the design.

"The Trump building has clearly used every trick in the book to maximize its size," she wrote. "But a great deal of care has also been lavished on its design. . . . It is undeniably a dramatically handsome structure."

Just as the then-new John Hancock Tower had done in Boston, Huxtable said, Trump Tower could bring Fifth Avenue "an airy dematerialization that combined surprising delicacy with a commanding presence.

"As this is written," she concluded, "the bargaining process for the Trump building is reaching its climax at City Hall."

Three months later, the commission voted unanimously to approve Trump Tower. It was a huge victory for the young developer. "I'm absolutely convinced," he wrote eight years later, "that it was the architecture itself that won us approval. And perhaps no one had a more powerful influence than Ada Louise Huxtable."

When it comes to gaining praise, Trump once even had time for George Will—a bow-tied columnist whose insights are quick, but who has been around long enough to become a true parody of himself.

"My favorite column on the world's tallest building came from columnist George Will," Trump wrote in 1987, after Will had praised Trump's plans as an expression of America's "brashness, zest, and élan."

"I've always liked George Will," Trump wrote, "in part because he's not afraid to challenge fashion."

By 2012, Will, however, had decided that Trump was "a bloviating ignoramus," and by 2016, Will had left the GOP over Trump's nomination. In true caricature form, the *New York Times* reported, "Will considered the matter [of the populist rise of Trump] over martinis at home that evening. The next morning, he walked into his [Georgetown townhouse] office and told his assistant: 'Go change my registration. This is not my party anymore.'"

The move raised questions over how exactly one's assistant can change one's party registration, but the love affair was certainly over. "George is a major loser," Trump told the cast of *Morning Joe* after clinching the states needed for the GOP nomination. "You know, he's a dour guy. Nobody watches him. Very few people listen to him. It's over for him, and I never want his support."

For most in the media, the relationship with Trump was less drastic, if more bipolar. Things can be easy-breezy, like when Tucker Carlson took over the 8 p.m. hour on Fox and President Trump called his cell phone to congratulate him on rising even faster than he himself had risen. Things could also be less breezy, like when, just a year prior at a rally ninety minutes outside Des Moines, I'd barely escaped while Trump campaign goons had herded a hapless Tucker into the reporter "cage," segregated from attendees.

And while Trump wouldn't hesitate to heap praise on one of our reporters or call on the *Daily Caller* in a press briefing, a mystified campaign hand told me that back in the day, the *Caller* had been on a banned media list alongside Trump's more liberal newspapers.

That, the aide told me, was likely the decision of Corey Lewandowski, Trump's thoroughly mediocre former campaign manager and likely one of the reasons Trump prefers to handle the press himself whenever possible.

From posing as his own PR flack in his early years to taking the stage to spar with the press, Trump has often shown he is his own best spokesman. In May, he eliminated his press secretary's daily on-air briefings, despite the ratings they garnered. He even floated potentially representing himself instead, once every two weeks.

Even while coming at him all day every day with allegations ranging from racism to being a Russian spy, "the opposition party" over at the *New York Times* has been honest enough to praise the access Trump has given them.

"Trump has frequently complained about my reporting, yet still got on the phone for an interview about his new life," the *Times*' Maggie Haberman tweeted in January 2017. "He remains the most accessible politician I've ever covered. It's why he did well with the tabloids in NYC [in the past], and what aided him in his 2016 campaign."

"I think one of the things that I think he's doing better than Barack Obama are these press conferences and his outreach to individual reporters, even for organizations, like my own, that he criticizes," said the *Times*' Glenn Thrush— a guy who was caught secretly working with Clinton campaign manager John Podesta while a reporter at the *Politico*.

"When Obama had press conferences, he had a single piece of white paper and he had six or seven organizations that he had preselected to call upon, and a lot of them were pretty favorable to him, too," Thrush continued. "I think Trump's free-ranging press conferences are a lot more democratic than the way that Obama conducted them."

Trump's own staff are barely able to keep up with the boss. When Bob Costa at the *Washington Post* broke news of one of the campaign's new hires, befuddled staffers wondered how Costa had known.

"The leaker in chief upstairs," a senior aide replied.

"President Trump called me on my cell phone Friday afternoon at 3:31 p.m.," Costa wrote on a different article months later, called "'Hello, Bob': President Trump Called My Cellphone to Say That the Health-Care Bill Was Dead."

When he loves you, you know it. When he doesn't, expect to hear the news break on the networks. And even then, the storm might pass quickly.

There are a few types of journalism in Washington, D.C. There's the really difficult reporting, when the subjects and sources don't want you to write the story. Then there's the reporting that gets done because a source wants it done.

Trump is a master of the latter.

And his mastery has not been completely lost on a press that is addicted to it regardless.

"It may not be good for America, but it's damn good for CBS," the company's president admitted. "The money's rolling in and this is fun."

Two employees at CNN told NPR that the company expected to make $100 million more than usual in the 2016 cycle—"thanks to the huge interest in Trump."

"CNN Had a Problem," the *New York Times* titled an article on the network's once-garbage ratings. "Donald Trump Solved It: Inside the strange symbiosis between Jeff Zucker and the president he helped create."

"I do get good ratings, you have to admit that," Trump trolled CNN's Acosta.

"I would be your biggest booster" if he thought CNN treated him better, he said. Of course, he already was their biggest booster.

It's true, much of the press hate Trump, but they need him. And it's true he has no love for them, but he needs them, too.

"While many in the press may disdain the way Trump uses them to rile up crowds and deflect from transgressions," the *Times* wrote of President Trump's relationship with the American media, "they know they have a rare story and a tantalizing, antagonizing protagonist."

And Donald Trump uses them. And it drives them batty.

You don't have to destroy some people. You won't want to destroy some people, even if you can. Others, you really simply can't. And then there's opting to use your opponents.

Washington, D.C., is full of people who think they're a lot smarter than they are. To see it up close is truly astonishing. Real America holds a little less of this instinct, but at work, in your community, on the school board or neighborhood committee, dumb folks acting smart are one of life's constants. But while they're the perfect subject for this kind of manipulation, a lot of intelligent opponents, competitors, and enemies can be worked around in a similar way.

If you fight everyone all the time, you won't get anywhere. Never forget that even the biggest pain in the rear can be an important resource. And if you want to have a little fun in the meantime, have at it.

RULE 22: If You Can't Use Them, Pour Water on Their Circuit Boards

"I would like to extend my best wishes to all, even the haters and losers, on this special date, September 11th."

That's the message Donald Trump sent out on his Twitter account at 7:21 a.m. on the twelfth anniversary of the worst terror attack in United States history. If it seems a little crude to you, imagine how it felt to "the haters and losers."

When he wants to, Trump just pours water on his critics' circuits and has a laugh while they spark and sputter. The Internet calls this "trolling," though Trump just thinks it's a bit of fun. And it's yielded some pretty impressive results.

"I could care less about the insults that Donald Trump gives to me," Jeb lied in the South Carolina primary debate. "It's blood sport for him, he enjoys it, and I'm glad he's happy about it. But I am sick and tired—I am sick and tired of him going after my family."

"My mom," he said a few seconds later, "is the strongest woman I know."

"She should be running," Trump replied without batting an eye. The audience in the room booed, but the Internet loved it and Trump was already leading the pack.

"Can you imagine Jeb Bush posting a video that suggests Marco Rubio is so boring he puts people to sleep?" the *Washington Post* asked after Trump released one showing a woman snoozing at a Jeb rally. "No. Trump can—and is willing to—say things that no one else in the race would ever dream of uttering in public. And so, Trump is always getting the last laugh."

And Jeb wasn't the only one to get trolled by Trump's sense of humor and his willingness to go beyond the lines other politicians adhered to.

He once suggested that Ted Cruz's Cuban father might be involved in the assassination of John F. Kennedy, even saying, "I mean, the whole thing is ridiculous."

Even chance seemed to side with The Donald's sense of humor when his Trump-branded plane flew so close to a Cruz rally they had to stop a moment just as Cruz was admitting he had lost.

"All right," Cruz said, laughing, "that was pretty well orchestrated!"

His ultimate troll move, of course, was reading Lindsey Graham's cell phone number out loud at a rally while riffing on how the fancier of South Carolina's two senators had given him the number to connect him with *Fox & Friends*.

"I think Rick Perry probably is smarter than Lindsey Graham," he added, trolling them both.

Politicians were not the only ones to fall victim to Trump's trolling, of course. He caught the media as flat-footed as the politicos.

"Do you mind if I sit back a little?" Trump asked Larry King on television as he sat for an interview in 1989. "Because your breath is very bad. It really is. Has this ever been told to you before?"

"No," King replied.

"Okay, then I won't bother," Trump said, cracking a smile and pulling his chair into the table.

"That's how you get the edge!" King exclaimed.

On January 27, 2016, Trump escalated his war on Megyn Kelly, tweeting, "I refuse to call Megyn Kelly a bimbo, because that would not be politically correct. Instead I will only call her a lightweight reporter!"

The following day, he retweeted a fan's picture of her *GQ* photo spread with the words, "And this is the bimbo that's asking presidential questions?"

In May, after burying the hatchet, he told her, "I have fans, you probably learned. . . . When you and I were having our little difficulty, you probably had some pretty nasty tweets sent your way. I don't want to say, but I heard that. I don't want that to happen."

"But you retweet some of those," Kelly shot back. "Not just the fans."

"Yeah," he conceded, "but not the more nasty ones. You would be amazed at the ones I don't retweet."

"Bimbo?"

"Uh, well, there was a retweet," he smirked. "Did I say that?"

"Many times."

"Ohhh, okay. Excuse me!"

And they both had a hearty laugh.

"You gonna stop that as president?" she followed up.

"Well, I'm gonna stop it about you now because I think I like our relationship right now."

"Democratic campaigns must stop looking at social media as a one-way communication device for amplifying over-produced campaign messages," an op-ed in the *New York Times* whined after Trump had won the general election. "The true power of social media for politicians is unleashed only if they use it to make emotional connections."

After the charred opponents and estimated billions of dollars in free coverage, Trump's long game culminated with a press conference to weigh in on President Obama's birth certificate.

Trump held the conference at the newly opened Trump Hotel in Washington, D.C. Once the cameras started rolling, he brought out a few dozen American veterans to tout his bona fides. Then, nearly forty minutes into every major station airing what was essentially a campaign ad, he said, "President Barack Obama was born in the United States. Now we all want to get back to making America strong and great again."

Then, he took the traveling press pool on a tour of his new property.

"In the expectation of them getting another scoop of Donald Trump saying something crazy, the media were treated to 40 minutes straight of war veterans endorsing Trump for president and a tour of his new Post Office hotel on Pennsylvania Avenue," reads a YouTube video called "The World's Greatest Troll: The Humor of Donald Trump."

"This was a dog and pony show for the Trump Hotel," CBS's Major Garrett fumed, visibly pissed. "It was also an effort by the Trump campaign to burnish Trump's image among those in the veterans community and the national security community, some of whom gave testimonials to Trump beforehand. But this was all staged to bring more attention to this brand-new hotel that Trump is opening here in Washington, D.C."

Pretty much dead-on.

"This was a completely invented event for the purpose of dropping this one-sentence declaration that Trump could have given at any moment at any time."

By living on American television screens—and in the

American media's heads—rent-free, Trump did more than dominate the news and have a good time; he pushed his enemies to practically self-destruct. Politicians like Rubio ended their campaigns making jokes about Trump's manhood. And the media began their postelection coverage wailing that Trump sneaking out to a steakhouse was a threat to the U.S. Constitution.

When he sneezed, pundits screamed fascism, murder, coup, tyrant. Bill Maher apologized for all the other Republicans he'd called an existential threat to America, because this time he was totally serious, you guys. The *Washington Post* changed its tagline to "Democracy Dies in Darkness," a title that would be cheesy on a Batman movie poster, and all Trump has to do these days is say "boo" and the press will run headfirst into a glass door.

So guess what: People stopped caring what the media said. And any freak-out, either real or imagined, was met with conservative opposition to his critics' perceived overreaction—a perception Trump was happy to play to.

"The fact is, no one has ever achieved anything significant without a chorus of critics standing on the sidelines explaining why it can't be done," Trump told Liberty University graduates at his first college commencement speech as president. "Nothing is easier or more pathetic than being a critic. Because they're people that can't get the job done."

It's not hard to wind up your opponents. Most of them will already be inclined to think the worst, so give them a spin. While they're panicked or overreacting, you can be sure they aren't thinking clearly about themselves, their goals, their strategy, or you. In the meantime, you just have to keep your eyes on the things that matter.

During a May interview with the Washington bureau chief of *Time,* a magazine people can apparently still buy in airports, he summed the endgame up perfectly: "Hey look, in the meantime, I guess, I can't be doing so badly, because I'm president, and you're not. You know. Say hello to everybody, OK?"

"Thank you very much, Mr. President," the reporter replied.

RULE 23: Don't Keep False Idols

Donald Trump has chased a lot of earthly things in his lifetime. Money, women, cars, planes, clubs, golf courses, and luxury, to name a few.

He's also chased a few projects that didn't end up working out. Things like Atlantic City gambling. Some among us might even remember "Trump Steaks," available "exclusively at The Sharper Image."

Win or lose, a constant in Trump's rise to success was a refusal to accept the common knowledge, or be constrained by the old rules. In his family business and political dealings, all idols were false—and he was determined to prove it.

He looked up to his father, Fred Trump, his whole life,

and Fred led the way into the real estate business for his son. Fred, who built his first house in the outer boroughs when he was still a boy, had made a fortune building affordable brick houses subsidized by the government's housing loans. He'd never entered business in Manhattan.

Donald Trump was never intimidated by his father, he writes, and had a "businesslike" relationship with him. He was, however, drawn by the glitz of Manhattan—even Manhattan at its worst, in the 1970s.

John Walter, Fred's nephew, recalled to the *New York Times* that Fred Trump would advise Donald, "This is nice and easy, what are you doing over there?"

While Trump was happy to give his dad's private-government business model a shot, *Business Insider* reports that "the government of New York City canceled the program in 1975—just as young Donald was about to get" started. And while he could have gone elsewhere, Manhattan was the goal—with or without the two pillars his father had built his empire on.

"You know, being the son of somebody, it could have been competition to me," Trump said lightly in an interview for his father's *New York Times* obituary. "This way, I got Manhattan all to myself!"

Today, buying cheap real estate in Manhattan makes all the sense in the world, but when he was getting started, they were cesspools, and the accepted wisdom was that suburbs are king.

In between 1973 and 2017, *Business Insider* reports, prices in the city went up a whopping 6,000 percent.

"And about five years ago," he told Tom Brokaw in 1980, "New York was not considered very hot and cities in general weren't considered too hot. . . . I like the inner cities, I see the inner cities as being sort of a wave of the future now. . . . I see the inner cities as being probably, in terms of real estate or in a real estate sense, probably the most viable investments."

Trump, who began his decades of contributing to the revitalization of New York City when he revitalized the failing Commodore Hotel in partnership with Hyatt, predicted on that show that within a few years, hotels could be going for as much as $1,000 a night in the city. By the time he was inaugurated president, the priciest room in the city commanded $75,000.

And these weren't the only idols he ignored in his rise—he also helped define a new sense of luxury in an old East Coast city used to catering to old money.

When he was building Trump Tower, he says, "The one market we didn't go after was old-money New Yorkers, who generally want to live in older buildings anyway."

Instead, Trump went a new way—toward the brash new money and after foreigners, including those who "didn't have the proper social references for [Manhattan apartment] cooperatives, or didn't want to put themselves through the scrutiny of a bunch of prying strangers."

And when his staff panicked that another new apartment

building was opening up just before Trump Tower and with significantly lower prices, Trump stayed the course: "The sort of wealthy people we were competing for don't look for bargains in apartments. They may want bargains in everything else, but when it comes to a home, they want the very best, not the best buy."

Of course, one of the country's biggest idols Trump tackled during his business career was when he bought a team in the United States Football League. In addition to realizing an American guy's dream of owning a football team, Trump writes, "I also liked the idea of taking on the NFL, a smug, self-satisfied monopoly that I believed was highly vulnerable to an aggressive competitor."

In the end, they lost, though the "smug, self-satisfied" NFL learned a few hard lessons along the way.

All this prepared him for the challenge of taking on the Republican establishment and all the idols it has held dear for decades.

While the myths of the D.C. GOP political establishment tend to be overstated—as Trump demonstrated so publicly—there is no doubt there's a core group of people and political platforms that govern the platform, and outsiders are often kept from positions of leadership.

One of the Republican Party's core traditions has been waiting your turn—something "Little Marco" heard loud and clear from the grand poohbahs when he dared challenge Jeb.

Think of it: After Reagan, it was his VP's turn. After

H. W. Bush, it went to party elder Bob Dole. H.W.'s son George W. Bush took his place, then it was time for John McCain, then Mitt's time to shine. And in 2016 it was Jeb! who would lead the GOP to victory with his massive war chest and elite pedigree.

To Trump, this meant nothing. And while guys like George Will wrote, "If Trump Is Nominated, the GOP Must Keep him out of the White House," Trump won the White House. (For his troubles, Will's Fox News contract was not renewed and he was cast down to choose his fate as either punching bag or GOP-basher on MSNBC.)

But beyond skipping the line—something a few have done before him—there were major tenets of GOP policy that no serious candidate had rebelled against since longtime conservative Pat Buchanan's primary against H.W. in 1992. Namely, the practically religious Republican devotion to free trade orthodoxy, corporate earnings, and democracy promotion.

When the North American Free Trade Agreement came along, billionaire businessman Ross Perot warned onstage that "there will be a giant sucking sound [of U.S. jobs] going south," but both major party nominees, Clinton and Herbert Walker, said yes. Clinton signed it, and no major candidate dared question for decades beyond.

Conservatives and libertarians alike have long praised free-market competition as the most efficient and moral economic system, citing centuries of data to back it up. Somehow, international trade was lumped in, and while politicos promised returns, Ross Perot's prediction came true and the long-ignored American working class was gutted.

Trump, a businessman and entertainer, is guilty of opportunism in his life. But "his view that trade [isn't] fair, that the world has long laughed at America and countries have taken advantage of U.S. generosity while refusing to pay their 'fair share' for all the U.S. does globally" has gone back decades, NPR reports (in that hushed and slightly annoying voice they love, no doubt).

"I was tired, and I think a lot of other people are tired of watching other people ripping off the United States," Trump told Larry King in 1987. "I believe it's very important that you have free trade, but we don't have free trade right now."

On foreign policy in the 2016 primary, candidates like Ted Cruz, Marco Rubio, John Kasich, Chris Christie, Carly Fiorina, and Lindsey Graham were aligned. Rand Paul and Donald Trump were not.

George W. Bush had called for a return to American interests in his run in 2000, but by 2003, with the invasion of Iraq, the entire party had swung around to using the military to promote democracy—even at the expense of fighting the country's enemies in Afghanistan.

And while the D.C. intellectual class flew into a panic, those ignored working-class voters, who were losing jobs to the economy and sons and daughters to foreign wars our enemies were winning, heard him. Twenty-five years of GOP orthodoxy was cracked.

"From this moment on, it's going to be America First," Trump declared from the steps of the U.S. Capitol—thirty years after the Larry King interview on trade. "Every decision on trade, on taxes, on immigration, on foreign affairs, will be made to benefit American workers and American families."

"That was some weird shit," George W. Bush reportedly giggled in the stands.

Republicans predicted Trump was doomed dozens of times on his climb to the White House, not only over questions of his civility, but over the agenda he espoused and the Republican idols he dispensed with.

The old guard had their chance and failed. And while Trump slammed their golden calves, horrified Republicans often cited the "Eleventh Commandment," which Reagan popularized in 1966: "Thou shalt not speak ill of any fellow Republican."

"The way I see it," Trump wrote in *The Art of the Deal,* "critics get to say what they want to about my work, so why shouldn't I be able to say what I want to about theirs?"

Ronald Reagan, of course, famously broke that rule when he primaried Gerald Ford, a sitting Republican president, in 1976. And more so, Reagan followed the Second Commandment, keeping no idols.

Idols are everywhere in the office. The "you can't do thats" and "it's never been done this ways." "Our grandfathers would roll over in their graves" if they saw a given forward-looking decision being made, goes the popular refrain, but in real life, it's more likely your grandparents would smack you silly for looking behind you while you're supposed to be driving forward.

That doesn't mean ignore tradition—an important word for the compounded wisdom of the men and women who have come before us. "Society," British statesman Edmund Burke observed quite correctly in the eighteenth century, is "a partnership not only between those who are living, but between those who are living, those who are dead, and those who are to be born."

But it does mean don't let yourself be held back by untested rules without reason. It means strive forward, always innovate, and always question why. You never know, maybe the widely accepted truth was simply never questioned. Find that false idol, question it, solve it—and win.

6

☆

How to Win So Much,
You'll Get Tired of Winning

He led the Jews out of Egypt and was pretty strict on false idols, but even mighty Moses learned there's no deal until you close it.

And the same goes for every one of us. Whether it's building the kid's tree house or building a world-class golf resort, making the biggest sale in your division or blazing a trail to the White House—if you don't win, it's a tough sell that you matter.

At the end of *The Art of the Deal,* Trump reports the outcome of the deals he was working on in the week of his life that he opened the book up with. Among them, his Atlantic City casino operation, the United States Football League, his planned move into Las Vegas, and his work on Mar-a-Lago. The only thing that links all four of these projects is that they were all projects Trump was working on in 1987.

Atlantic City, while succeeding for a number of years, would end up being a sore spot on the campaign trail, when laid-off employees and wronged landowners featured prominently in attack ads and debates. The *Washington Free Beacon*'s Bill McMorris was the lone reporter on the scene in October 2016, the once-glittering Taj Mahal casino's final day—until he was kicked to the boardwalk by a pit boss who didn't like his cigarette, his camera, or his questions.

The USFL, of course, is nowhere to be found—though its players still dot the Pro Football Hall of Fame and ESPN's evening lineup.

Las Vegas didn't come to pass that year, though today, Trump International Hotel towers over the skyline, off the main strip.

Mar-a-Lago, meanwhile, has assumed the role of "Winter White House." Foreign leaders visit frequently, world-altering decisions are made on its deck, and a helipad has just been installed for Marine One—the presidential helicopter. At the beginning of Trump's first year as president, the initiation fee doubled from $100,000 to $200,000 for the first time since 2012, when Bernie Madoff bankrupted a good chunk of the patrons.

All were impressive ventures. All had an impact on him and the people around him. But it's the deals he closed and the wins he put up that matter in the end.

If you come up one state short, you're a loser. But in win after win after win, overcoming the losses, learning from them, and soldiering on, Donald Trump showed the world he knows how to cross the finish line in style.

And while any one of us can credit a win here, or blame a loss there, on someone else in the chain making the right or wrong call, when the day is done, the most important player to winning in your own life is yourself.

RULE 24: Your Best Business Partner Is Always Yourself
Donald Trump trusts his brand. Day in and day out, he, his associates, and his campaign used Trump products—and on the campaign trail, he touted it.

The lifelong New Yorker's long climb to the presidency began with a slow descent on one of the golden escalators that line the three-hundred-foot-tall atrium of Trump Tower.

He based his campaign there, too, just as he had his company. He housed his comparatively small staff in unfurnished levels of the building and often ate at the Trump Tower Grill—the same grill he famously plugged in his Cinco de Mayo taco-bowl trolling.

Trump's campaign offices, like most offices, also stocked bottled water. And while the president loves Coca-Cola products so much, he has a "red button" installed on his Oval Office desk for when he wants to order one up (and prank his visitors), everyone knows that Coca-Cola's water brand, Dasani, tastes like it was bottled in Flint. So the campaign spent $3,000 on Trump ICE—a water bottle that is served only at Trump Tower, in Trump restaurants, on Trump golf courses, and at Trump hotels. Trump ICE made The Donald more than $400,000 in 2015 and has its own Wikipedia page (though it is shorter than Dasani's).

He was generous with the water, too, once sending "Little Marco" a case of it along with some "Make America Great Again" towels—"for him sweating," as the campaign told CNN.

It wasn't just products. Trump never missed an opportunity to speak at one of his properties, either. It must have been among Tony Blair's more emasculating moments when he was cut short midsentence in June 2016 while he talked to Fox about the recent British vote to leave the European Union.

"In respect to Syrian refugees," the former British prime minister was saying in his pitch-perfect C-3PO voice, "we have the perfect right, because we're not part of the full European system—"

"Hey, Mr. Prime Minister?" *Fox & Friends* host Steve Doocy interrupted after looking at his phone.

"And we have a perfect right," Blair continued, "to decide who comes into our country and who doesn't."

"Uh, pardon the interruption, Donald Trump is up in Turnberry right now," Doocy said as Blair blinked. "He's taking some questions from the press, and they have questions on Brexit."

And like that, Tony Blair was shoved aside and forgotten in favor of a half hour of Donald Trump. For the next thirty-three minutes, wearing a white "Make America Great Again" hat, he answered reporter questions on Brexit, outdoors at his rugged Scottish golf course, while the networks played it into American homes.

Good advertising, if you can get it.

"I have very successful companies," he announced in a March 8 speech touting primary wins that night. In the minutes after, while the cameras rolled, Trump touted Trump's Mar-a-Lago ("100 percent by me with no debt"), Trump's golf resort ("where we just had the major championship"), Trump's beachside buildings ("very successful"), Trump's New York City projects ("one of the most successful projects ever built in real estate"), Trump ICE ("we have water and it's . . . very successful"), and Trump Steaks.

"And by the way, if you want to take one, we'll charge you about, what, fifty bucks a steak.

"We have *Trump* magazine," he continued, and Trump Shuttle airline, Trump University, Trump Vodka, and, of course, Trump Winery.

"I mean there's nothing like it. Close to two thousand acres. It's in Charlottesville, Virginia. Right next to the Thomas Jefferson memorial. And we're very proud of it. We make the finest wine. As good a wine as you can get anywhere in the world, and I know the press is extremely honest, so I won't offer them any, but if they want, they can take a bottle of wine home.

"And so, I just want to—so I wanted to put that to rest," he said, beginning to wrap up a thirty-minute infomercial played on national television free of charge.

Fast-forward a few months and CBS's Major Garrett could barely contain his rage, as Trump wrapped up a presser at D.C.'s new Trump Hotel and offered reporters a guided tour of the building.

Trump didn't simply rely on his own goods for the sake of profit. It also kept him in his comfort zone while campaigning.

Trump likes his home and his own restaurants. He prefers to live and eat at home in Trump Tower, but when campaigning his countless properties provided a home away from home.

Relying on his own business empire helped the Trump campaign run a lean operation. When *USA Today* crunched the Federal Election Commission numbers on the final spending on Trump property, they concluded, "President Trump's campaign spent a total of $12.7 million at businesses run by him and his family members over the course of the 2016 presidential election."

Or, in the breathless words of often-breathless *Daily Beast,* "Donald Trump Is Paying Himself to Run for President."

The claim, of course, is preposterous. Trump donated $66 million to his own campaign. At the risk of stumping the enterprising reporters who uncovered this story, it's worth asking how, exactly, Trump made a buck on this campaign.

But turning a profit wasn't the point. Despite the hysterics and a few good laughs, Trump wasn't on the campaign trail to sell water or hotel rooms—he was trying to sell himself. And if his campaign wouldn't avail itself of his hotels, his food, his water, his plane, and his golf courses, why should anyone bother to vote for him?

Mitt Romney, like many politicians before him, ran from the wealthy characterization, terrified it would make him appear out of touch. Instead, he appeared disingenuous and inhuman. If he was proud of himself and what he'd done, why would he run from his own record? If he wasn't proud of his business record and the private car elevator it let him buy, what reason did voters have to make him chief executive?

Trump didn't make that mistake. He thought he made the best of everything, and told voters as much.

As president, though, Trump was given a new retreat he could call his own: Camp David.

Camp David was built in the woods of Maryland's Catoctin Mountains by Franklin Delano Roosevelt's New Deal government labor force. Originally built as a vacation spot for government workers and their families, Roosevelt decided he liked it and took it for his own use. He made it a presidential retreat and called it "Shangri-La" (the current name was coined by Dwight Eisenhower).

FDR hosted Winston Churchill there, and every president since has hosted major foreign dignitaries in its wooded privacy. Until Donald Trump.

"Yea, Camp David is very rustic, it's nice, you'd like it," Trump told the *Times* of London. "You know how long you'd like it? For about thirty minutes."

Trump prefers Mar-a-Lago, Trump Tower, and a golf club in New Jersey's fox-hunting country. And he's fairly brash about it.

The same goes for entertainment: something Trump has rarely outsourced.

Madonna, Lady Gaga, Bruce Springsteen, and the Roots are among just a few acts who worked their butts off to bring crowds to dance at Hillary Clinton's rallies. Lacking an exciting message of her own, Clinton tried simply hanging out with the cool kids and hoping it would make her cool, too.

On the day before the election, tens of thousands of people gathered in Philadelphia for Hillary Clinton's final round of rallies. This one featured Bruce Springsteen, Bon Jovi, both Obamas, and Bill Clinton. What's the chance some of those people weren't there for Hilldog? A reporter for the *Philadelphia Inquirer* frankly observed that the biggest ovation of the night wasn't for Clinton; it was for Michelle Obama.

The cool set didn't want to hang out with Donald Trump (except for Kid Rock, who is awesome). And some of his warm-up acts, folks like Jerry Falwell Jr., so completely lacked charisma it was painful to witness.

After his helicopter and his airplane, which he used to

buzz crowds and get people excited, all Trump had was his words. And with those words, he filled the rooms.

"You need to generate interest, and you need to create excitement," Trump writes in *The Art of the Deal*. "One way is to hire public relations people and pay them a lot of money to sell whatever you've got.

"But to me," he continued, "that's like hiring outside consultants to study a market. It's never as good as doing it yourself."

It's rare to have your own airplane. It's also rare to have famous bands play while you make the case for your product or promotion to your client or boss, so we're just going to have to do without. But we all have our own product, from our personal presentation to what we've created at work to what we bring home to our families. If you don't believe in it, who will?

Why cite the Internet when you can cite your own study? Why go to outside counsel when you have the ability to save the company or your family money and do it yourself? There's no doubt it's more impressive. That is—and this is important—if your own product is solid. Before you can sell something, you have to make it, and while confidence will get you far, you'll need quality to keep it going.

When he first started running for president, people had a laugh at the helicopter rides, fiery speeches, and good humor. It was all a sideshow—until Donald Trump started to win states.

RULE 25: People Won't Take You Seriously
Until You Win

No matter what you think of yourself, when you walk into a room the only thing people care about is what you accomplished. Brash, that's fine, but explain your worth with your actions. Just look at who Trump respects and doesn't respect (it's not hard, he doesn't hide it). To be a lifetime politico in his orbit is to be in a precarious place: If you haven't accomplished something real on this earth, he's not impressed.

When Donald Trump first arrived in Manhattan, determined to make his mark, his first move was to join Le Club. Of course when he first called, no one knew him from Adam. And the same for the next time. Only through confidence, persistence, and resourcefulness did he get his foot jammed into the doorway long enough to make an introduction anyone could remember.

And here was his chance. Brash and young, he sold himself hard, and in the process made friends and, of course, a few enemies. But friend or enemy, interactions with the young Donald Trump left enough people to matter wondering, Who the hell is this kid?

It would be important to show them, and right quick.

Trump saw his first big chance in 1973, when the Penn Central Railroad went bankrupt, leaving plots of land in need of a buyer at a time when New York City was far from a desirable locale. The man they trusted to sell them was Victor Palmieri, making Victor a man Donald Trump wanted very much to meet.

"I called his representative," Trump writes, "and said, 'Hello, my name is Donald Trump and I'd like to buy the Sixtieth Street yards.'"

Courage was Trump's path through the door. It's true, his successful father across the river could back him, and his family had spent years cultivating political ties in a city where real estate ran on them, but there were many people with far more money and clout than a kid barely out of college.

"I hadn't built anything yet, but what I did have was the willingness to go after things that people in a better position than mine wouldn't have considered seeking," Trump recalled.

First and second, Trump laid out all the problems he would face developing the property: problems with the local community, as well as problems with the government and zoning board.

"The third thing I did, and probably the most important," he writes in *The Art of the Deal*, "was to sell myself to Victor and his people. I couldn't sell him on my experience or my accomplishment, so instead I sold him on my energy and my enthusiasm."

Victor saw something he liked. Decades later, he recalled to Virginia's *Politico* magazine that Trump "was not the most agreeable personality I had ever met." He was, however, "someone who was young, who was very knowledgeable about New York politics—and particularly the politics governing zoning and tax abatements"—all things necessary to moving this land.

"He's almost a throwback to the nineteenth century as a promoter," Victor explained to a *Barron's* reporter who asked why Trump had gotten the deal. "He's larger than life."

Others were less impressed.

"Trump has a great line of shit, but where are the bricks and mortar?" one big dog asked, in a comment that got back to a man who was as easily incensed then as he is now. And when he heard it, Trump was about as angry as you might expect. Without any solid wins under his belt, he knew, that "great line of shit" was his "Trump card"—and he'd better win the hand.

"I remember being outraged when I heard that, and I didn't speak to this guy for more than a year," he recalls of the incident. But the big dog was right, and Donald knew it.

"It could have all gone up in smoke," he wrote, looking back over a decade later. "If I hadn't managed to make one of those first projects happen, if I hadn't finally convinced the city to choose my West 34th Street site for its convention center and then gone on to develop the Grand Hyatt, I'd probably be back in Brooklyn today, collecting rents."

In short, he had to win.

His first win was complicated, and not total.

It took a lot of time and money to sell the city government on building a convention center on Thirty-Fourth Street, and

THE ART OF THE DONALD ★ 225

when, after two mayors, Trump finally did in 1978, he was not awarded the contract to build it. He'd sold the property and won a tactical victory, but the loss of the contract was bitter.

And there were losses, too.

In 1979, an inability to get financing forced him to let go of his options to build on the Sixtieth Street yards. The land was bought by a wealthy Argentinian builder who didn't have Trump's local connections or savvy, and eventually failed as well.

But Trump refused to quit.

Trump put the resources from the Thirty-Fourth Street win, plus his now-developed relationship with Victor, into his first major victory: the Grand Hyatt hotel renovation— the win that vaulted him from Donald to The Donald.

He then swooped back in and bought the Sixtieth Street yards from the man he'd sold them to years earlier.

People were starting to take Donald Trump seriously.

And in the end, it wasn't because of what he said. What he said got him noticed, but Trump took off because he was able to deliver.

"You can't con people," Trump writes. "At least not for long. You can create excitement, you can do wonderful promotion and get all kinds of press, and you can throw in a little hyperbole. But if you don't deliver the goods, people will eventually catch on."

That is about as simple as it gets. Our mothers might give

us a hug when we're little kids because we tried because they simply love us, but by the time we're adults, the people who love us—even Mom—often need us, too. It's the adult world, and bills aren't paid with good intentions. Everything, from presentation to sale, dress to confidence, comes crashing down when there's no delivery.

Every single thing we ever did to get in the door will come to naught if we don't deliver.

Trump's last great win in New York came in 2016, at the same Thirty-Fourth Street site he'd been denied so many years before. Without Trump's involvement, the city had forged ahead with sticking a convention center on the plot. Unlike so many Trump projects, the new center was finished late and went millions over budget. When completed, the heinous glass monstrosity was named the Javits Center.

In 2016, in a jab at Trump, Hillary Clinton chose the Javits Center—and its massive glass ceiling—to host her presidential victory party. The night of the election, I led a Daily Caller News Foundation film crew through throngs of beta males and hipster girls, all gathered at the site of one of Donald Trump's first deals and first disappointments, to see the businessman defeated once and for all.

But it wasn't Trump who would see defeat that night. Hours later, the same betas and hipsters were streaming from the Javits Center in droves. Some sobbed, some wandered aimlessly like shell-shocked survivors, and others simply sat on the ground and curled into a ball.

It looked like, after forty years, the Thirty-Fourth Street yards would be the scene of Trump's big win after all.

"Sorry to keep you waiting, folks," the president-elect greeted a crowd a little farther uptown. "Complicated business!"

RULE 26: Don't Throw Money at Your Problems

Donald Trump wasn't supposed to win.

After gleefully admitting that the Republican Party had chosen Donald Trump as its candidate, the *New York Times* reported, "Donald J. Trump dominated the Republican presidential primaries with relatively little money and few staff members. As his campaign shifts to the general election, some of his allies and donors have raised concerns about whether such a lean operation can effectively compete against Hillary Clinton, the presumptive Democratic nominee."

By all counts, they had a point. History is the best guide to predicting the future, and larger, deeper-pocketed campaigns tended to make a difference in close contests.

Jeb! Bush had done it the way it was supposed to be done. He gathered the country's top Republican consultants. He tapped his family's decades-old fund-raising network. He toured the country, speaking at fund-raisers that ranged from twenty-five dollars a ticket to six figures per seat. He created a super PAC called Right to Rise, which amassed more than one hundred million dollars to spend on advertisements. He warned Mitt Romney he'd outraise him (scaring Romney off another run), and warned Bush allies not to sign on with anyone else. He announced his run with a display that, if it wasn't carefully crafted by outside consultants with the help of focus groups, certainly felt like it was. He hopped onstage in a blue collared shirt (Look serious, but not too stiff or formal!), thanked the crowd, feigned surprise at their excitement (Oh, what humility!), and showed due deference to his mother (family values!) by asking her to get the crowd seated.

Hillary Clinton went the same route. Seven months before the election, she had ten times the campaign staff her opponent did, and had spent millions more.

What good it did her. Even with a budget many times his, and a media largely in her corner, Trump spent more time on Americans' televisions and newspapers.

When we were splitting up coverage zones the night of the Iowa caucuses, I chose wrong, heading to a highway-side Sheraton hotel, where Trump had set up a cash bar behind the Secret Service lines where foreign correspondents, local supporters, armed men, and girls dressed for the club could mingle.

"I'd wondered if Trump would serve champagne," I joked, but he didn't get rich from throwing money away.

Trump was never one to shy from lavish parties and high-priced expenses—but that was in pursuit of things that cost a lot of money. Politics, he wagered, shouldn't. Volunteers, earned news coverage, old friends, and existing party structure, those were his preferred weapons. Weren't those things, he reasoned, the exact things his opponents were spending hundreds of millions to get anyway?

"I believe in spending what you have to," Trump wrote in the 1980s. He learned to watch how his father built low-income housing—quickly and affordably. "I learned from my father that every penny counts, because before too long your pennies turn into dollars.

"To this day, if I feel a contractor is overcharging me, I pick up the phone even if it's only for $5,000 or $10,000, and I'll complain.

"The day I can't pick up the telephone and make a twenty-five-cent call to save $10,000," Trump writes, "is the day I'm going to close up shop."

Why spend money when you have the resources to do it yourself with hard work and some good thinking?

"The consultants that suck up all that money," President Trump told a crowded room of conservatives a month after his inauguration. "Oh, they suck it up, they're so good. They're not good at politics, but they're really good at sucking up people's money. Especially my opponent's, because I kept them down to a minimum!"

When a young Trump was busy renovating the Grand Hyatt with his father as a prominent backer, "the older man kept tabs on the job site and dispenses builder lore," Gwenda Blair writes in *The Trumps: Three Generations That Built an Empire*—"including his practice of adding a bucket of water to every bucket of paint in order to stretch it."

"According to his sons," his *New York Times* obituary reads, "he would routinely drive his Cadillac to one of his many construction sites after the day's work was over. Wearing a natty suit—with his chiseled features and wide grin, he resembled a silent-film star—he would walk through the studs and across the plywood floors, picking up unused nails to hand back to his carpenters the next day."

It was a lesson he worked hard to instill in his children, but like a lot of boys, Donald Trump was determined to learn the hard way.

A little over a decade later, in 1991, Trump found out what spending too much could do.

Politico magazine, hardly a fan of Mr. Trump, Candidate Trump, or President Trump, nevertheless hit the mark in one title: "1988: The Year Donald Trump Lost His Mind."

That year, characterized by a lot of very expensive deals for flashy investments that had a hard path to profit—an airline, a famous hotel, and a yacht—found the forty-one-year-old businessman up to his neck.

Trump's lavish spending in the late 1980s and early '90s left him overstretched, and by 1991, four years after he had published *The Art of the Deal* and in the midst of an expensive divorce from his wife, Ivana, Trump's Taj Mahal casino filed for Chapter 11. He lost the yacht, the airline, half his stake in the Park hotel, and the Taj.

It hurt, and it was embarrassing, but using a lot of the lessons herein, Trump survived.

By 1997, when he published *The Art of the Comeback*, he'd renegotiated his debts, gotten back in the saddle, and learned a few lessons—at age forty-five, he finally recognized his father's wisdom on the importance of pennies.

"I'm running a business," Trump said in a June interview on the difficult decisions he had to make in those years, "for myself, for my company, for my employees, and for my family."

The experience left him determined not to break the bank in a big, self-aggrandizing presidential run.

A few of the tough lessons Trump learned are, no doubt, familiar. We've spent too much, racked up some debt, had to let go of things we cherished, and been embarrassed by decisions we made and lessons we didn't pay enough attention to. Picking ourselves up, learning from these errors, and keeping our money in our pockets when there's a thousand reasons—but no good reason—to throw it away are the kinds of habits that lead to success in building a business and a life.

Whether it's building a business empire or buying political ads, the common wisdom is often to spend, spend, spend. It's not true, and many a fool goes bankrupt following this maxim. Once, nearly Trump himself.

But he's not famous for his business losses, and if we're hardworking, a little lucky, and successful, when our eulogies are written it's the victories that will define us.

But business isn't everything in this life.

Even if you're Trump.

How to Live the Best Life

"I don't do it for the money," Trump wrote in the first sentence of *The Art of the Deal*.

"I've got enough," he continued, "much more than I'll ever need. Deals are my art form. Other people paint beautifully on canvas or write wonderful poetry. I like making deals, preferably big deals. That's how I get my kicks."

It was a theme he'd echoed since a young man. In 1980, Tom Brokaw asked the thirty-three-year-old Donald what his goal was—did he want to be a billionaire? "No, I really don't," Trump replied in a fashion we're less used to seeing these days. "I just want to keep busy and keep active and be interested in what I do. That's all there is to life as far as I'm concerned."

Whether you adore him or despise him, it's undeniable that Donald Trump has fun. He has for decades. Singing onstage, clowning around in movies, traveling the world in search of the best golfing, chasing beautiful women. And unlike most of us, who would cause all kinds of trouble at home living a life like this, every one of his kids loves him, talks to him, and, for the most part, works with him.

How many billionaires can claim that? How many normal families can even claim that?

Most of us aren't twice divorced. But when we saw Donald Trump hosting ex-wife Ivana's latest wedding at Mar-a-Lago, and saw both ex-wives in attendance at his inauguration, it was hard not to wonder if his divorces are more amicable than many people's marriages.

Before business, before making money, before succeeding in a career, there's life itself. Donald Trump is living proof that no matter if you're up or down, it's the ride that counts. Enjoy it.

RULE 27: Eat Like a Normal Person

"Happy Cinco de Mayo!" Trump tweeted the May before the election. "The best taco bowls are made in Trump Tower Grill. I love Hispanics!"

The press tantrum was nearly immediate. They realized he was trolling them, and yet they still couldn't help themselves.

A writer at Vox, a website where thoroughly mediocre minds lecture readers on current events, called the tweet "shocking" and tried to fact-check it by looking over menus for Trump Tower restaurants. The bowl, they breathlessly relayed, was more likely sold by Trump Cafe than Trump Grill. Big scoop.

Benny Johnson, a journalist who lives to troll venerable dumpsters like Vox, noticed Trump's desk had an old picture of Marla Maples in a bikini.

"What Trump did was so insensitive," a by-then-defeated Jeb Bush whined to a European newspaper. "First, not all Hispanics are Mexican. Secondly, not all Hispanics eat tacos. Thirdly, showing your sensitivity by eating an American dish is the most insensitive thing you can do. Fourthly, to say this, next to all things he already said, is a further insult. It's like eating a watermelon and saying 'I love African-Americans.'"

The Verge, a tech site, noticed there were no vegetables: "There is just fried tortilla, salsa, cheese, meat, and a scoop of sour cream.

"I think I might see a single bit of chopped tomato in the top left corner, and a sprig of cilantro," the reporter continued. "Or maybe that's a trick of the lens, the Sun reflecting off Trump's fork to create the illusion of nutrition."

Most of America saw a pretty funny tweet.

Most Americans eat tacos or nachos on Cinco de Mayo without thinking twice about whether it's offensive. Most Mexican restaurants cater to it and rake in the cash.

Most American men don't mind a quick bikini pic with their lunch break. And a ton of us eat at our desks, too.

Finally, plenty of us forget (or "forget") to eat our vegetables.

In an age of stifling political correctness and gluten-free juice-cleansing, the Republican nominee's tweet pierced through all the garbage to the regular human beings he wanted to vote for him. It was authentic.

Ted Cruz staffer Brian Phillips was correct when he joked online that the first mistake Trump made was eating Tex-Mex in New York City (as opposed to, say, Austin, Texas), but the image still stood in stark contrast to the lack of relatability in old Ted "For Human President" Cruz.

And it was just about the polar opposite of John Kerry asking for Swiss at a Philadelphia cheesesteak shop.

"I rarely stop for lunch," Trump wrote a few decades before. And true to form, in almost every picture of Donald Trump eating lunch, he's on the road or at his desk. Domino's in the office, KFC in the airplane, Big Macs on silver platters, Mars Bars in the Oval Office, and the omnipresent Coca-Cola Classics.

"I have never seen a thin person drinking a Diet Coke," he joked in 2012. And today, he enjoys trolling visitors to the White House with a red button. "With the push of a red button placed on the Resolute Desk that presidents have used for decades," the Associated Press reported, "a White House butler soon arrived with a Coke for the president."

"Chris, you and I are going to have the meat loaf," he told fellow candy lover Governor Chris Christie at a White House dinner, before the two dug into one of America's most iconic, if misunderstood, dishes.

In May 2017, CNN devoted two whole segments to how Trump got two scoops of ice cream at dinner while other guests were given one.

There was no word on whether Jeb!, who had gone on a paleo diet to lose weight and make voters like him more, found the ice cream incident insensitive.

"A little more moderation would be good," Trump once admitted. "Of course, my life hasn't exactly been one of moderation."

He's "a red-meat guy," Axios wrote on his eating habits. "Trump loves big steaks, preferably the ones served at his clubs."

Some of Trump's culinary habits are a little more questionable. Habits like steak well-done and served with ketchup. But in fairness, how many of our grandparents share a similar taste for their beef?

While even acknowledging that a full quarter of the country prefers their steak this way or similar, the executive editor of *Eater* wrote a nearly two-thousand-word essay using the steak temperature to conclude that since it's Donald Trump, the results could "be catastrophic."

But then, the American press corps is known for neither self-reflection nor understanding the tastes of the rest of the country.

"When President Donald Trump sits down for dinner in

Saudi Arabia, caterers have ensured that his favorite meal—
steak with a side of ketchup—will be offered alongside the
traditional local cuisine," the Associated Press sneered in the
opening line of a story on the president's first trip abroad.
It took some work, but reporters were able to contort their
angles well enough to make it seem that a foreign power
doing everything it could to make the U.S. president comfortable was a bad thing. The trip, we now know, was a re-
sounding success.

But the reality is despite the gold and other luxuries he
surrounds himself with, Donald Trump's taste in food is
shared by a lot of guys from Queens, and if the president of
the United States showed up in your town today and asked
for dinner, you'd probably be able to serve up something he'd
love—or at least swing by a drive-through.

And people don't begrudge it. Why would they?

The relatability of eating like a normal American tran-
scends politics. While Hillary Clinton struggled to pour a
beer in Wisconsin, her way-more-likable husband was known
for sneaking off to McDonald's at the end of a jog.

Fancy food can be fun, junk food can be terrible, and the
total reverse can be true at any moment, too. Stay open to
new things, but never close the door on taking a break from
the day to enjoy the things you really enjoy.

Bill and Donald had another point in all that junk food,
though. If you want to eat like a man, you'd best exercise like
one, too.

RULE 28: Exercise Like a Man

Donald Trump is no gym rat. You won't see him lifting weights with Paul Ryan or jumping rope with Barack Obama.

Aides say he has no hobbies besides golf. He doesn't hike or hunt, as his sons do. Trump's pleasures revolve around work.

He's not going to be challenging Arnold to a benching competition (though he'd happily take part in a ratings contest).

He might be willing to take on former Senator Harry Reid in an exercise band contest, though after nearly losing his eye the old Nevadan might want to stay away from that move himself.

Nope. When Donald Trump wants exercise, he does what most American males his age and a lot of younger men and women would much prefer—he heads to the golf course. His own, naturally.

The golf course fits basically every aspect of Donald Trump's personality. He gets out in his club, he gets to take part in some competition, and he can even make a few deals while he's at it.

"The only workout Trump gets is an occasional round of golf," Axios fretted. "On the campaign trail he viewed his rallies as his form of exercise."

He's not alone. The majority of Americans aren't hitting the gym to work out inside. Planet Fitness, NPR whispers in its annoying way, has an average of 6,500 members per gym—gyms that can accommodate about three hundred people, typically. Planet Fitness can pull this off only because most of us don't really show up that much. We're busy, or prefer to get our exercise another way. Or we're working—two things that can be combined on the course.

In 1858, the *New York Atlas* newspaper published a thirteen-part series called "Manly Health and Training" under the name "Mose Velsor." The real author was one Walt Whitman, the manly American writer. It includes such patriotic sections as "Meat as the Principal Diet for the Inhabitants of the Northern States" and "The Great American Evil—Indigestion," peppered with advice the president (and a good deal of the rest of us) might agree with, such as "Let the main part of the diet be meat, to the exclusion of all else."

But there's also a lot to be said for the importance of the outdoors. "Out-Doors," he writes. "In that word is the great antiseptic—the true medicine of humanity.

"Places of training, and all for gymnastic exercises should be in the open air—upon the turf or sand is best," Whitman continues. "Cellars and low-roofed attics are to be condemned, especially the former."

"After two health obsessed, workout warriors as presidents, Trump marks a return to a 90s-era, Middle America Bill Clinton diet," the reporters at Axios observed, but it also marks a return to an America more like, well, America.

It's good to take care of the body. It's also good to keep track of what's important in life. And being comfortable in your own skin is a big part of that.

The country's elites in both politics and the media were amazed that Donald Trump was able to reach around them and excite Americans. He didn't have a lot of the same problems Americans have. He didn't have to save money to make sure he could buy his kids new hockey equipment, stop eating out to afford a family vacation, or put off repairs on his car—the kinds of things that most of us have to deal with all the time.

Of course, neither did the American elites, in either politics or media. In fact, Trump was a heck of a lot more like us than any of them were. His detractors were missing something. They saw a guy like Mitt Romney, who couldn't identify with someone so low as a factory owner, and they assumed America's rejection of Romney was some sort of affirmation of the eternal class war they're so obsessed with waging. It wasn't.

We don't really care if someone's rich. In fact, most people think it's pretty great, and the ones who aren't rich now sure hope they are someday. It's the matter of liking someone—of actually liking someone—that makes all the difference in the world.

People liked George W. Bush. They liked Bill Clinton. They liked Ronald Reagan. They liked John F. Kennedy. And while it looks rough on the TV, a lot of people legitimately like Donald Trump.

If you're true to yourself, chances are people will like you, too. When you aren't, we can tell.

Still, another question remains for his mystified opposition: How did the New York billionaire who led the populist rebellion do it all while wearing a suit?

RULE 29: In Dress, Combine Understated Elegance with Branded Flair

"Controversy, in short, sells," Donald Trump wrote in *The Art of the Deal.* "So, it turned out, did glamour."

At least most of the time. And when it doesn't, Trump has always paid close attention.

Harvey Myerson died in February 2015, just four months before Donald Trump ran for president. If you google his name, you'll see sad headlines about a fall from grace for a man who was once one of New York City's most famous lawyers. But in the mid-1980s, he was still riding high, making his name on clients like Trump and cases like Trump's suit against the NFL.

"Harvey is an incredible trial lawyer," Trump wrote at the time. "He took [the *United States Football League v. NFL*] case in which no one gave us a prayer going in, and he managed to win on antitrust grounds, even though we were awarded only token damages.

"Even so, I wondered, since the trial, whether perhaps Harvey was just a little too sharp for some of the jurors," Trump continued, darkly foreshadowing the high-rolling,

Rolls-Royce lifestyle that would eventually bring Harvey down. "Every day he'd show up in one of his beautiful pin-stripe suits, with a little handkerchief in his pocket, and I'm just not sure how well that went over."

It seems a near-prophetic observation, given the way Harvey's life would unravel in just the next few years. Or maybe Trump had caught a whiff of rotten on his cologne.

The observation stands out dramatically in a book that also devotes paragraph after paragraph to the importance of picking the finest marble for the finest lobbies. And it shows a lot about the businessman's situational awareness that his critics would not care to give due credit for.

Donald Trump nearly lives in a suit. If you search online for "Donald Trump not in a suit," "Donald Trump casual," or any number of those combinations, the results are insignificant—and all are in a collar on the golf course.

Even in his family picture with Melania and their son, Barron, Donald Trump is wearing a solid blue tie.

Scott Adams, the *Dilbert* cartoonist who gained some notoriety and lost a lot of friends for his blog complimenting Trump's ability to persuade people, wrote, "Trump's language and imagery is all 'big and beautiful and great.' His buildings are big and powerful. Trump is a big guy in a power suit wearing powerful clothing. He projects power, intentionally."

Fashion websites have tried to trace Trump's style to Gordon Gekko's in the movie *Wall Street*. Gekko's wardrobe, which the studio spent $50,000 on, was described by the designer as "f--- you clothes."

Well, maybe that means "power, intentionally." But *Wall Street* came out in 1987, and if anyone bothered to take a look at Trump in '86, '85, '84, they'd see the same style: typically blue suits, white shirts, and shiny red ties.

Maybe it's all a little more simple than his critics would like to let on. Maybe he's comfortable in this clothing. Maybe that's actually exactly who he is, which is why he's so darn comfortable.

When I dodged his goons in a high school gymnasium in rural Iowa, a few types of people stood out. One, the reporters, in jackets and ties (I ditched mine in a bathroom). Two, Trump's campaign staff, nearly all short and fat or tall and skinny, in terrible suits out of a 1991 mobster movie. And three, the crowd, where it was not unusual to see a man in a Vietnam War hat, Vietnam War shirt, Vietnam jacket, and jeans.

And then there was Donald Trump, in a blue suit, white shirt, and bright tie, somehow fitting in with the crowd more seamlessly than any of us coastal scribes and wannabes.

In New Hampshire, where the crowd's uniform was puffy winter coats, snow boots, and jeans, the same. While other candidates, constantly worried about how they looked, would roll up their sleeves, go tieless whenever possible, and make fun of each other's boots, Trump simply dressed how he wanted, and it worked.

He even wore a blue suit, white shirt, and white trucker cap to hand out flood supplies in Louisiana.

"When Donald Trump ran for president he put his clear, simple message on the front of bright red hats," Adams blogged. "The message was perfect. The choice of a hat instead of a t-shirt or other garment was perfect. The color red was perfect for his message—bold, sexy, and important. The hats were a master class in branding and influence.

"Political historians," he concluded, "will be referring to Trump's hats for ages."

But what good is a hat if you can't wear it? Donald Trump, Manhattan real estate magnate, has never run away from a hat, be it a bright pink golf hat or a camouflage trucker hat. While politicians from Calvin Coolidge to Michael Dukakis to Paul Ryan have been mocked for putting on an Indian headdress or cute little cap (remember how quickly Jeff Sessions took off his MAGA hat?), Trump has worn multiple colors.

And Coolidge, to his credit, calmed his distraught advisers, reasoning, "Well, it's good for people to laugh, isn't it?"

Democrats were shocked that a billionaire in a fancy suit could get the attention of America's working people, but no added attention to style was going to make these same working people decide they loved Hillary Clinton.

While Hillary Clinton took heat for her $12,000 Armani jacket during a speech on inequality, and Sarah Palin took heat for her $150,000 campaign clothing budget, Trump led the populist charge with a trucker hat and a Brioni Italian business suit, and there's a lesson to it.

- Keep your ties simple, and possibly of your own design.
- Use tape if the short end goes wild in the wind.
- They say the first rule of campaigning is "don't put on the hat"—but you're breaking the rules, so wear the hat all the time.

In truth, none of these rules apply to us, but there's one that does: Be yourself. Work for the job you want to have (as opposed to the one you have), dress professionally whenever you're in public, but don't BS and don't wear a costume, or your peers will see right through it.

Be yourself, because we really do know when someone isn't.

And love what you do.

RULE 30: Love Your Job

Donald Trump is a worker.

Folks in the media, who often fake concern while wondering how a man who allegedly works so hard finds time to golf as often as he does (more than any other president), miss the point. To them, golf is something they might hit after work—and only after every other hobby they enjoy outside of work has been exhausted.

For President Trump, not so much. It's work, family, and golf. Nothing else, really, except television, which for Donald Trump is work. Meaning, the times you hear about Donald Trump golfing—and that's going to be every time he does, these days—are really the only times he isn't working. And he famously goes to bed late and wakes up early.

Sort of puts some perspective on how often he's working.

But even in the office, Trump is not your traditional worker.

"I try not to schedule too many meetings," he wrote in *The Art of the Deal*. "I leave my door open. You can't be imaginative or entrepreneurial if you've got too much structure. I prefer to come to work each day and just see what develops."

It's a strategy that has taken some getting-to-grips in the White House, but in the business world, people were always amazed at the access they had to the boss. On a Friday in the first chapter of his first book, he described catching up on the news, starting at 6:30 a.m.; an on-site project presentation with city planners at 9:15; a meeting with the architect and top executives of another building back at Trump Tower at 10:30; a follow-up meeting on the work that goes in before the construction at 11; a call on a hotel acquisition at noon; an ad selection at 12:15 p.m.; Nevada gaming license forms at 12:30; a look at a school he was considering sending a then-young Ivanka to in the fall at 12:45; a call with a local contact at 2:30; a meeting with the guy building his own apartment at 2:45; a call with "a Greek shipping magnate" at 3:30; a conversation on buying a plane at 4; a call on a potential casino deal at 4:30; and then, at 4:45, a call from his assistant that David Letterman was in the atrium showing some tourists around New York on camera. Letterman, she said, would like to visit.

Sure, Trump says, admitting he's not a regular viewer—too late at night, "but I know he's hot."

After some fun conversation and a look around the office, Letterman comments, "It's Friday afternoon, you get a call from us out of the blue, you tell us we can come up. Now you're standing here talking to us. You must not have much to do!"

"Truthfully, David," Trump says, "you're right. Absolutely nothing to do."

Plenty of folks assume Trump does it all for the money. There's no doubt some truth to money as a motivator, though Trump has protested, "Money was never a big motivator for me, except as a way to keep score."

And there's also something to his love of what he does. Something that drove him in good and bad times, that would no doubt drive him if he were far less successful than he is, and something that drove him to seek the presidency of the United States—a fairly thankless, poorly paying job compared to the life he put on hold.

"The real excitement," as Trump tells it, "is playing the game."

Before you have a family and a mortgage—in other words, before you're an adult—there's nothing more important than loving your job. Except for having one, that is, as there's little more pathetic than that guy sitting in Mom's basement griping that he just can't find a job he likes enough to work.

But the quickest path to fulfillment isn't some dream gig with easy hours and no boss. That, my friends, is likely not right around the corner, unless you're about to happily and securely retire. The tricks to taking joy in your work are many, but two central tenets are to enjoy your field, and what you do for it; and, most important, to know why you're working, and take meaning from it.

It isn't always easy to love your job. But even if you don't, it's essential to love your work. You might work at a giant sales company you know will lay off your division if you're guilty of selling too much merchandise (which means big payouts from the top), but if you love to sell, it's a reason to get up. Besides, if you're good at it, you'll land on your feet.

A lot of those bosses can be hell, but if you love to dive into code or get greasy in an engine for a living, you'll find your path to daily satisfaction no matter the field.

Take joy in what you do, and as soon as you don't, look for a way to quit that won't leave your bills in a lurch. When you love the deal, when you love your work, it shows, and people will recognize it.

But most important, know why you work. We aren't material creatures at heart, us humans. We are spiritual animals who have been looking toward the skies since we took shelter in caves. Since the days we kept warm by fires, and everywhere in the world people still do, we people yearn for far more.

We don't just work for our bosses and our bank accounts, we work for ourselves, for our parents, for our kids, for our husbands and wives. It's not just grinding it out for a pension or a retirement fund, it's building a career—and a life around it—so that we can look back with pride and think, I may not be president or have my own TV show, but I mean everything to the people I've built this for.

We make deals because we need to. And in love, sports, and work, winning means more than just a few bucks—it means our world.

"I don't kid myself," Donald Trump admits. "Life is very fragile, and success doesn't change that. If anything, success makes it more fragile.

"Anything can change, and without warning," he continued, "and that's why I try not to take any of what's happened too seriously."

Live and love your life, never lose sight of what's important, and never ever lose track of what winning is.

You won't go wrong.

✯

The White House Challenge

Donald Trump has never faced a challenge like he faces in the White House.

People often say it's the hardest gig in the world, though when you're working eighteen-hour days in a job where you need to shower off after, that's tough to buy. But consider this: There's a sprawling U.S. government with nearly three million federal employees and one and a half million military personnel making decisions every day. Among all those men and women, only the hardest decisions that a) no one can make, or b) no one wants to make, land on the president's desk.

In addition, you can't go to most public places, do have to travel all over the world, are scrutinized on every single thing you or anyone close to you does, and can't even tie on a decent drunk (not that this bothers the teetotaling president).

The White House is also completely different from any

operation he's ever run. Donald Trump famously ran a lean firm, but now the operation he runs is sprawling. In addition, they're not his people. Indeed, there are few workforces outside of Hollywood's Screen Actors Guild more opposed to an agenda of cutting or reforming government. And unlike reality TV or the business world, it's hard to fire people.

The result has been near-constant leaks to a press that thinks he is a threat to the country. Every week, "current and former administration officials, who asked to remain anonymous," attack the commander in chief, leaking sensitive and mundane materials that garner sensationalist headlines.

Leaks at the Trump Organization weren't unheard-of (Trump made plenty himself), but the climate in the White House is different: Almost every current and former member of the executive branch can use leaks to create front-page news on whatever topic they wanted.

If Donald Trump is brought down at the top of his game—from the top of the free world—here's why, and what we can learn from it.

"My father's scene was a little rough for my tastes," Trump said. "In this business," one rent collector told a young Trump, "if you knock on the wrong apartment at the wrong apartment at the wrong time, you're liable to get shot."

But even after he left the boroughs, Trump had competitors who desperately wanted to defeat him. Rough men who would lie and make threats; people who would leak to the press in an attempt to help their business and hinder his.

But little in the world of business—even construction and casinos—can prepare someone for ascending to the highest target in the world.

In his first term as president, he isn't simply the target of foreign actors intent on sowing chaos in the American government—he is the target of a political party with unlimited access to the media, aided by a largely sympathetic press corps. He also has to cope with universities, Hollywood, Silicon Valley, and Wall Street, all of which are dominated at the top by men and women who don't just oppose Trump, but in many cases loathe him. His opponents are more numerous than at any previous point in his life.

Donald Trump will also likely be the last president of the United States to make his bones before the Information Age.

While he built his name on television and built his campaign on the twenty-four-hour news cycle, he built his business empire—the source of his wealth and experience—before smartphones and social media even existed.

Before the days of near-instant information gratification, Donald Trump was his own publicist, calling reporters who met with their peers in person and used tape recorders to try to figure out whom they'd been talking with.

In those days, Trump made a lot of hay in dealing with ambiguity. He became a master of the shell game. What is real? What isn't? Would he build the tallest building in the world? Would he open a casino in Vegas? Was the line he gave a concrete position or the opening salvo of a public negotiation? Who did you trust, the papers or the TV? *National Review* or the *Washington Post*?

In this information gap, Trump was able to operate with a great deal of authority, even when employing a little playful exaggeration to move stories he was pushing from the middle of the paper to the front page.

The year Donald Trump was inaugurated president of the United States may have been the most triumphant year in the businessman's life, even while the ability to instantly verify a pitch made it the toughest year for the art of the deal.

And when a live-streaming news media actively opposes your agenda, it's easy for misinformation to spread. And never before have his tweets had such a swift and profound impact on his reality.

Like a story from the *Politico,* a self-important website based in Virginia, that the Ku Klux Klan was distributing beer and drugs in black neighborhoods to slow Democratic voting. That story was clearly false, yet spread like fire because it fit into the media's laughable fear that around every corner was a secret cabal of white supremacists with torches ready to stop their girl Hillary.

Or the story from a difficult-to-tolerate website called *Slate,* which asserted that Donald Trump had a secret Russian Web server. That story was picked up by the leadership of the Democratic Party, including Hillary Clinton and Harry Reid, and spread across the country through the Internet until the FBI called BS the following day.

And then there was the portion of the press that said Hillary Clinton was in fine health and it was sexist to question it. That is, before she collapsed in public after an hour in mild New York weather.

And then a story picked up by allegedly respectable portions of the media that Trump might be in "cognitive decline," based on the unseemly musings of doctors who had never had the president as a patient—an obviously unethical undertaking. Diagnosing someone you've never met is "one of the most difficult topics for any journalist to take on," one impressed reporter mused without any tinge of self-awareness.

Earlier that very week, every major newspaper in the country had carried the story of Trump's proposed "Medicaid cuts," despite Medicaid spending going up every year under the White House budget.

The list of stories reporting ominously on standard occurrences, or highlighting one set of facts while excluding another, could fill a hall of records—all while these same reporters breathlessly complain about an apparent phenomenon of "fake news" in support of the president.

In addition to an army of opponents in the media, the United States, and the world, Donald Trump's nominal allies, the Republican Party, are more numerous, less loyal, and less under his command than any group of captains he has ever led.

The Trump Organization is led by a combination of family and executives hired on by Trump or brought up through the ranks from the golf course or bodyguard position to the top. He values trust, time, good decision making, and other such things in these men and women, and they reward him for it.

But the Grand Old Party is another thing entirely. After years as a Democrat, then third-party man, Trump didn't spend the decades in the trenches that professional political operatives value. Those years, spent instead in business and entertainment, are a huge part of what endeared him to the voters—but it's a harder sell to "the swamp."

His slash-and-burn tactics in the primary changed the way we look at modern politics, but did not win him friends among the professional political class, which projects an aura of toughness yet has its feelings hurt quite easily.

And finally, while huge numbers of blue-collar voters turned out for Trump in Pennsylvania, Michigan, and Wisconsin, breaching the Democrat's "blue wall" and sealing Hillary's doom, in states where Republicans were reelected, embattled politicians often found they had more votes than Trump earned at the top of the ticket.

That indicates that the usual presidential "coattails" that lower-rung politicians can ride to victory didn't appear. Trump, it seems, is a one-man army, explaining why his sometimes bumpy ride didn't affect their polling numbers, and gave them less need to support the man.

Will they defend their commander in chief the way Democrats and the media defended President Barack Obama with accusations of racism, kidnapping, and even terrorism when Republicans attacked? So far, it looks like Trump is on his own.

Not that it's so surprising, of course. Politicians of all stripes bill themselves as leaders, when really they follow the winds of favor more slavishly than any cartoon yes-man.

It's a new world for Donald Trump, and one he's in charge of. But every time he stumbles, he learns, just as he learned how to deal with the press, not to back his loans with personal money, and who his real friends were when he was down.

He's new to this, and entering a new world of interaction in your seventh decade is a tough learning curve, but he isn't new to setbacks—even drastic ones. He's been knocked down, even thought to be knocked out. Business "experts" thought Trump was finished in the early 1990s. Political "experts" thought he was finally finished about a dozen different times, but Donald Trump has proven to be a very tough kill.

Even through divorce, near-personal bankruptcy, and the loss of control over some of his most public assets, Trump learned hard lessons and rose to the next challenge, becoming even more famous, more wealthy, and more powerful.

The drive—the killer instinct—described in this book, combined with his love of the game, always propelled him forward.

The problems of a besieged presidency in an instant-information age aren't the kinds of problems most of us will ever come across. It's a rare day that our enemies have such incredible access to the public and our company is in open rebellion against us. Still, the principles in this book—the principles that have guided Donald Trump's life—are the kind that can act as a guide through most any storm life winds up.

The higher you climb, the harder the game.

Live a good life, follow your own path, and make the deal. The level we're dealing at, and the business it's in, well, that's just going to have to come down to us.

Acknowledgments

Thank you to Blake Neff, Tucker Carlson, Geoffrey Ingersoll, Martin Avila, Mitchell Ivers, Keith Urbahn, Matt Latimer, Vince Coglianese, James McCrery, Katie Frates, and my friends and family.

Acknowledgments